PAT BROWN, MBA

Financial Literacy For NIL for High School Student Athletes

"Your Game Plan for Earning, Saving, and Building Wealth Before College"

ABRAM 47 BROWN

First published by AbramBrown47 2025

First edition

ISBN: 978-1-967737-04-8

This book was professionally typeset on Reedsy.
Find out more at reedsy.com

Contents

Introduction: Why This Book Matters

If you're reading this, chances are you're a high school athlete with big dreams. Maybe you're already making a name for yourself. Maybe your highlight tapes are circulating on social media. Maybe your inbox is buzzing with interest from college coaches, agents, or even brands. Wherever you are on your journey, there's one thing you need to know:

The game has changed.

You're not just an athlete anymore—you're a brand. You have the power to earn money from your *Name, Image, and Likeness* (NIL). That means sponsorships, social media deals, merchandise, camps, appearances, and more. NIL is opening doors that didn't even exist a few years ago. And it's exciting. But it can also be confusing, overwhelming, and—if you're not prepared—risky.

That's where this book comes in.

Why NIL and Financial Literacy Go Hand-in-Hand

When I was your age, there was no such thing as NIL. I played football at the University of Kansas, served as a team captain, and even went on to play professionally in Canada. But if NIL had existed back then, I would have been completely unprepared for it. Nobody taught us how to manage money, how to read a contract, how to protect our image, or how to say no to a bad deal. We were just focused on winning games, passing classes, and hoping to go pro.

And I'll be honest—when I did start making money, I made some mistakes. I didn't know how taxes worked. I didn't understand budgeting. I trusted people I shouldn't have. I wish I had someone to guide me.

That's why I wrote this book—for you.

You're growing up in a time where NIL is creating real financial opportunities for teenagers. But money without education can lead to chaos. If you don't understand how to manage it, save it, invest it, or protect it, NIL can become more of a trap than a blessing. This book is designed to help you avoid that trap and set yourself up for long-term success—on and off the field.

NIL Isn't Just for College Athletes Anymore

Just a few years ago, NIL was something only college athletes had access to. But now, thanks to changes in state laws and school policies, *high school athletes* in many states can take advantage of NIL opportunities, too.

That means you could:

- Get paid to promote products on Instagram or TikTok
- Start your own clothing line or training camp
- Appear at youth sports events or autograph signings
- Partner with local or national brands
- Be treated like a business—while still in high school

But with these opportunities come responsibilities. You're now stepping into a world where contracts, taxes, agents, and branding all matter. That's a lot for any teenager to handle. And unfortunately, not everyone has your best interests at heart. This book will help you make smart decisions and surround yourself with people who do.

Why Financial Literacy Is a Game-Changer

Let's break it down: *financial literacy* means understanding how money works. It means knowing how to budget, save, spend, invest, and avoid debt. It's about learning how to make your money work for you—not just today, but for the rest of your life.

Here's the truth: most people don't get taught this stuff. Not in school. Not at home. And definitely not on social media. That's a big reason why so many people—athletes included—end up broke even after making a lot of money.

This book is here to change that.

You don't need to be a math genius. You don't need a million dollars. You just need the right mindset and some basic tools. If you learn these skills now, at 16 or 17, you'll be light-years ahead of your peers—and even some adults.

Who This Book Is For

This book is for:

- High school athletes who already have NIL deals
- Athletes who are just getting started and want to be prepared
- Parents and guardians who want to support their kids
- Coaches and mentors who want to protect their players
- Anyone trying to make sense of this new NIL world

Whether you're a five-star recruit or just getting varsity minutes, you need to understand how to manage your brand and your money. NIL opportunities may come quickly, but the knowledge in this book will help you build a legacy that lasts.

What You'll Learn

This isn't just another NIL rulebook or a boring financial textbook. It's a playbook—a practical, real-world guide tailored for high school athletes like you. Here's just some of what you'll learn:

- How to create a personal brand that opens doors (without selling out)
- What to look for—and look out for—in NIL contracts

- How to manage your money like a pro (even if it's just $100/month)
- What taxes mean when you're getting paid (yep, you gotta file)
- Who to trust (and how to tell when someone's running game on you)
- How to think long-term, even if your dream is to go pro
- How NIL fits into your college goals, future career, and bigger purpose

And maybe most importantly—you'll learn how to be confident with your decisions. You'll know when to say yes, when to say no, and how to stand on your values.

Why You Should Care—Even If You're Not Making Money Yet

Let's say you're not getting NIL offers yet. Should you still read this book?

Absolutely.

NIL is about more than money. It's about mindset. It's about how you carry yourself. It's about understanding the business of being an athlete, and positioning yourself for opportunities when they come.

The habits you build now—how you budget, how you save, how you treat your name—will impact your future far more than any single deal ever could. This book gives you those habits and helps you build a strong financial foundation, whether NIL becomes your income today or five years from now.

Final Thoughts

The world of NIL is still evolving, and high school athletes like you are right at the forefront of this new era. That means there's both opportunity and responsibility in front of you—opportunity to earn, grow, and build a foundation for your future, and responsibility to make informed, strategic decisions that protect your interests.

This book isn't about chasing quick money or hype. It's about helping you understand what's really at stake—your name, your reputation, and your financial future. Whether NIL becomes a major part of your life or just a small chapter in your story, the knowledge and tools in the pages ahead will serve you well far beyond sports.

The decisions you make now will shape the way you handle money, business, and personal branding for years to come. If you approach NIL with the same discipline you bring to training, school, and competition, you'll be in a strong position—no matter what comes next.

Let's get into it.

Why NIL Matters Earlier Than You Think

A lot of high school athletes assume NIL is something they'll worry about once they get to college. But the truth is, NIL starts impacting your life way before you sign a letter of intent. Here's why:

1. Your Brand Is Already Being Built

Whether you realize it or not, every post, highlight video, interview, and even classroom interaction contributes to your personal brand. College coaches, brands, media outlets, and even fans are paying attention earlier than ever. If you're active on social media, you already have a platform—and that means you're already shaping your image.

2. Opportunities Are Showing Up Sooner

More and more states are allowing high school athletes to sign NIL deals. And even in states where it's not officially allowed, athletes are still being recruited with NIL conversations in the background. Some high school athletes are getting paid to promote products, host camps, or sell merchandise. This isn't the future—it's already happening.

3. Decisions You Make Now Can Affect Future Deals

A tweet today could cost you a deal tomorrow. A bad financial habit now could lead to bigger problems later. A poorly managed NIL opportunity could create legal or eligibility issues. Laying the right foundation now protects you later when the stakes are higher.

4. NIL Is About More Than Just Money

Sure, NIL involves income—but it also teaches entrepreneurship, professionalism, and financial responsibility. Getting familiar with things like contracts, taxes, budgeting, and brand management early gives you a major head start. Whether you go pro in sports or not, these are skills you'll use for the rest of your life.

5. Colleges Are Watching

College programs are increasingly looking at recruits who understand how to handle themselves on and off the field. If you show you can manage your NIL presence maturely, that can give you an edge in recruiting conversations. Coaches want players who bring value—not just in athletic performance, but in how they represent the school.

Bottom line: NIL is already part of the game at the high school level. Waiting to take it seriously is like waiting until college to start training—by then, you might already be behind. Start learning now, and you'll be ready for every opportunity that comes your way.

The Intersection of Money, Sports, and Opportunity

For decades, high school sports have been seen as a stepping stone—a pathway to a college scholarship or, for a select few, a professional career. But with the arrival of NIL (Name, Image, and Likeness), that traditional path is expanding. Suddenly, the intersection of **money, sports, and opportunity** isn't reserved for college or pro athletes anymore—it's happening right now, at the high school level.

And it's reshaping the game.

Sports Is No Longer Just About the Scoreboard

When you step onto the field, court, or track, your goal is to win. But in today's world, what happens *off* the field is just as important. With a phone in your hand and a following on social media, you have the power to market yourself, connect with brands, and turn your athletic platform into a business—before you ever sign a scholarship or play in a televised game.

Athletes are no longer just athletes. You're a brand. A business. A potential influencer. And that means the decisions you make today—about your image, your money, and your message—can create real opportunities, or real consequences.

When Money Gets Involved, Everything Changes

Let's be clear: NIL isn't just about getting paid to post on Instagram. It's about entering the world of financial responsibility, taxes, contracts, decision-making, and in some cases—pressure. Whether your first NIL deal brings in $50 or $5,000, the moment money enters the picture, everything gets more complicated.

- Who's advising you?
- Who's getting a cut?
- Are you paying taxes?
- What does that contract *actually* say?
- Will this deal hurt your eligibility?

These are questions adults struggle with—and now high school student-athletes have to navigate them, too. That's why financial literacy is no longer optional. It's essential.

Opportunity Is Everywhere—If You're Ready

Here's the exciting part: NIL creates opportunities that didn't exist for the athletes who came before you. You can:

- Start a business or launch a brand
- Get paid for what you're already doing
- Build relationships with local companies and community leaders
- Gain real-world experience with contracts, marketing, and entrepreneurship

But not all opportunities are created equal. Some deals sound good but come with strings attached. Others are designed to take advantage of young athletes who don't know better. The key is being able to tell the difference—and that's where knowledge becomes your greatest advantage.

The New Reality

The intersection of money, sports, and opportunity is your new playing field. It's not something to fear—it's something to prepare for. NIL isn't a distraction from your goals—it can be a tool to help you reach them. But like anything in sports, success requires training, awareness, and the right mindset.

This book is part of your NIL training camp. Let's get to work.

Pat's Personal Story and Why He Wrote This Book

I grew up in a small Midwestern town, raised in a hardworking household where money wasn't something we talked much about—because there usually wasn't much to talk about. I went to school with kids who came from wealthier families, kids who got new cars for their 16th birthday while I was just hoping for a ride to practice. That early exposure to financial differences planted a seed in me—even though I didn't know it yet.

Sports became my path. I played football at the University of Kansas, eventually earning the honor of being a team captain. During my time there, we were nationally ranked, and I even went on to play professionally in the CFL for the Calgary Stampeders. On the surface, it looked like I had "made it." But behind the scenes, I was still figuring out what so many student-athletes quietly wrestle with: how to handle money, how to understand contracts, and how to protect my financial future.

No one taught us this stuff.

In college, I took a financial literacy class designed for student-athletes—and it rocked me. I realized quickly how much I *didn't* know. While some of my teammates were already managing family trusts or investment portfolios, I was learning basic budgeting and how credit works for the first time. It was eye-opening and humbling. But instead of feeling ashamed, I got curious. I leaned in. That class changed the trajectory of my life.

After football, I went into financial planning. I became a wealth manager and have now spent over two decades helping people make smart financial decisions. But I never lost sight of where I came from—or who I was doing this work for.

Then NIL came along.

When the NCAA and state governments started changing NIL rules, my phone started ringing. Former teammates. Coaches. Parents of athletes. Everyone had questions—most of them the same: *"How do we do this right?"* That's when I knew there was a gap that needed to be filled. High school athletes were suddenly in a position to earn money, sign deals, and make grown-up decisions—but very few were being given the tools to do it wisely.

I thought back to my younger self: a high school athlete with big dreams but no roadmap. I thought about how a single bad financial decision—even one made out of excitement or ignorance—can have long-term consequences. I thought about all the talented young athletes out there who deserve better guidance than a random DM from someone claiming to be a "brand rep."

So I wrote this book.

This is the book I wish I had when I was your age. It's not about getting rich quick or chasing flashy deals. It's about *understanding the game behind the game*—so you can play it smart, play it legally, and set yourself up for success both now and in the future.

Whether you go on to play college ball, go pro, or hang up your cleats after high school, the lessons in this book are meant to last a lifetime. NIL is just the beginning, but money decisions never stop. This book is your playbook to handle it all with confidence.

How to Use This Guide Year-by-Year

Whether you're just starting high school or heading into your senior season, this guide is built to grow with you. NIL doesn't follow the same timeline for everyone—some athletes start getting offers early, others later. Some states allow NIL in high school, others don't. No matter your situation, you can use this book as a playbook to prepare, protect, and position yourself for success.

Here's how to approach it year by year:

Freshman Year – Laying the Groundwork

Your first year is all about setting the tone. This is the time to focus on building strong habits both on and off the field.

What to focus on:

- Learn what NIL actually is and how it might affect you down the road
- Start being intentional about your social media and personal image
- Understand how money works—budgeting, saving, and spending
- Set some early goals (on the field and financially)

Why it matters:

Even if NIL isn't on your radar yet, building good habits now will make everything easier when the time comes.

Sophomore Year – Building Your Platform

This is the year to level up your presence and your mindset. You're growing as an athlete—and your brand can grow too.

What to focus on:

- Continue shaping your reputation and online presence
- Explore local opportunities or NIL-friendly programs, if available
- Start tracking your money, even if it's just allowance or a part-time job
- Get your family involved in understanding NIL and financial decisions

Why it matters:

This is the year where visibility increases. As you improve athletically, make sure your finances and personal brand are improving too.

Junior Year – Getting NIL Ready

Junior year is often when serious attention starts coming your way—recruiting, offers, showcases, and even NIL possibilities.

What to focus on:

- Learn how to recognize legitimate NIL opportunities
- Get comfortable reading basic contracts and understanding what you're agreeing to
- Understand how taxes work on NIL income (yes, even in high school)
- Start identifying adults who can help—mentors, coaches, family, or trusted advisors

Why it matters:

This is when a lot of mistakes happen—signing bad deals, trusting the wrong people, or mishandling money. Being prepared now can protect your future.

Senior Year – NIL Smart and Decision Ready

This is the year where things get real. Whether NIL deals are coming in or not, you're about to make big decisions about your future.

What to focus on:

- Polish your personal brand—make sure it reflects who you are
- Be smart about offers—don't just say yes because it sounds good
- Know how NIL might impact college admissions, scholarships, or financial aid
- Think long-term: where is this NIL journey taking you beyond high school?

Why it matters:

This is your launchpad into adulthood. Even if NIL hasn't been part of your journey yet, the financial habits and awareness you've built will help you in college, your career, or whatever path you choose.

Tips for Making the Most of This Guide

- Don't feel like you have to read everything at once—flip to the sections that apply to where you are now
- Use the checklists, templates, and examples throughout the book to stay organized
- Revisit sections as you grow—what didn't apply last year might be relevant now
- Share what you learn with teammates, family, and friends. This isn't just about you—it's about building a culture of smart, empowered athletes

NIL is changing fast, and the athletes who succeed will be the ones who treat it like a business—early. No matter what year you're in, you can use this guide to make confident, informed decisions and take control of your future.

How This Book Connects to the Full NIL Financial Literacy Series

This book, *Financial Literacy for NIL for High School Student-Athletes,* is not a stand-alone manual. It's part of a comprehensive educational series built to support student-athletes and their families at every stage of their NIL journey—from high school through college, from early exposure to NIL opportunities to long-term financial growth and independence.

If you're reading this book, it likely means you're curious about what lies ahead—not just in sports, but in life. You want to understand how to prepare for NIL the *right* way—before the money starts coming in, before the offers roll in, and before decisions start stacking up fast. This book was created to help you do just that. It's about building your mindset, your money habits, your brand, and your ability to handle opportunities responsibly—years before you're officially in the game. But to fully benefit from this learning experience, it helps to understand how this book fits within the larger NIL literacy blueprint.

The flagship title in the series, *Financial Literacy for NIL,* is written for college student-athletes and advanced high school students preparing to take that leap. It offers direct financial education for athletes already managing NIL income—covering everything from handling self-employment earnings and avoiding scams to understanding taxes, LLCs, and investing. It speaks directly to athletes navigating contracts, agents, branding, and building a long-term financial plan. While that book helps athletes manage NIL while they're in the thick of it, this high school edition is designed to prepare you *before* any of that happens—before you sign anything, before you feel pressure to perform, and before NIL expectations feel overwhelming.

Financial Literacy for NIL for High School Student-Athletes is focused on early preparation. It's designed to help you understand the basics of money, mindset, and personal brand development. You'll learn how to budget and save, how to build a digital presence with purpose, how to navigate peer pressure, and how to start thinking like a business—even as a teenager. This book meets you where you are, whether you're just starting high school or heading into your senior year. It provides a framework for making smart decisions now, so you're ready to lead when opportunity knocks later.

This book also ties directly into *Financial Literacy for NIL for International Student-Athletes*, which is designed for athletes competing in the U.S. on visas like F-1, CPT, or OPT. That edition addresses unique challenges like cross-border banking, tax reporting, and navigating NCAA compliance rules with immigration in mind. Even if you're not an international student, understanding your teammates' experiences and how NIL plays out globally can help you build smarter partnerships and a more inclusive perspective.

Finally, this series includes *Financial Literacy for NIL for Parents of Student-Athletes*. That guide is written specifically for your biggest supporters—your parents, guardians, and mentors. While you're learning how to manage NIL from your perspective, the parent book helps them understand what you're learning, what you're up against, and how to guide you through it all without overstepping. When both you and your family speak the same NIL language, communication gets easier, decisions get clearer, and success becomes a shared goal.

Think of these books like a team: this high school edition is your strength coach, getting your foundation solid; the college edition is your game-day coordinator, helping you make smart moves under pressure; the international edition is your compliance coach, guiding you through complex systems; and the parent guide is your sideline mentor, always in your corner. Together, they form a complete system to help you succeed not just in NIL—but in life.

You don't have to figure it all out alone. This series is here so you—and your support system—can grow together, plan ahead, and handle every step of the NIL journey with confidence. Because when NIL is done right, it's not just a short-term win. It's a long-term game-changer.

Chapter 1: Build the Right Foundation

FRESHMAN YEAR: Start Smart, Start Early

High school is a fresh start. New classes, new teammates, new competition—and if you're an athlete with talent and drive, new eyes on you. College recruiters, coaches, and now, even brands and businesses may be paying attention to what you say, do, post, and represent. It might not feel like it yet, but your freshman year is the beginning of something much bigger than four years of school sports.

This chapter is about planting seeds. It's about preparing early so that by the time NIL (Name, Image, and Likeness) opportunities come knocking—or flooding—you're not overwhelmed or unprepared. You're ready.

Let's walk through what you need to know, do, and think about as a freshman athlete in this new NIL world.

What Is NIL, and Why Should You Care Now?

Let's keep it simple: **NIL stands for Name, Image, and Likeness.** It refers to your right as an athlete to profit from your identity and marketability.

This includes:

- Getting paid to post about a product on Instagram or TikTok
- Hosting a youth skills camp in your hometown
- Selling a t-shirt with your logo or nickname

- Signing autographs or doing a paid appearance
- Partnering with local businesses or national brands

At the college level, NIL is already booming. And now, in many states, **high school athletes are allowed to participate in NIL deals, too**. Even if your state hasn't caught up yet, it's just a matter of time. NIL is expanding quickly—and you need to be ready before the opportunities arrive.

Why now? Because NIL isn't something you can just "figure out later." The athletes who succeed with NIL are the ones who plan, learn, and build early. That means you, as a freshman, have a huge advantage: **time**. Time to prepare, time to grow, and time to learn the business side of being an athlete.

The NIL Reality Check

Here's what a lot of student-athletes don't realize: NIL is about more than just money. It brings new responsibility, pressure, and visibility. If you're getting paid to represent a brand, you are no longer *just* a student or athlete. You're part of a business agreement—and businesses expect professionalism.

That's why you need to understand things like:

- Contracts: What are you agreeing to?
- Taxes: Did you know you'll owe money on NIL income?
- Time management: Can you balance school, sports, and NIL work?
- Reputation: Will brands want to work with you based on your image?

These things sound heavy, and they are. But learning about them now, before the spotlight is on you, puts you way ahead of the game.

Your Brand Begins Now

Whether you have 100 followers or 10,000, you already have a personal brand. Every post, video, tweet, and comment says something about who you are. NIL success is often tied to how well you manage your image—and it starts much earlier than most athletes think.

Here's what to do this year:

- **Clean up your social media**. Go back and delete anything negative, inappropriate, or immature. You never know who's watching.
- **Be consistent with your message**. If you say you value hard work, show it through your actions—on and off the field.
- **Engage with your audience**. Thank people who support you, highlight teammates, and be a positive presence.
- **Be intentional**. Before you post, ask: "Does this align with who I want to be and how I want to be seen?"

The brand you build now could lead to NIL deals later—or cost you those deals if you're careless.

Goal Setting: More Than Just Stats

Everyone sets athletic goals—better times, more points, stronger lifts. But freshman year is the time to go deeper. Set goals that help you become a more complete person.

Here are some areas to set goals in:

- **Academic**: GPA targets, study habits, improving in tough subjects
- **Athletic**: Skill development, strength, team leadership, consistency
- **Personal Brand**: Growing your online presence, volunteering, networking
- **Financial**: Saving money, tracking spending, avoiding impulse buys

Sample Freshman Goals:

- "I will maintain a 3.5 GPA to stay NCAA eligible and attract scholarships."
- "I will post once a week about my training or community involvement."
- "I will save $20 per month from my part-time job or allowance."
- "I will not post anything online I wouldn't want a college coach or sponsor to see."

Writing these goals down and reviewing them monthly creates discipline—and NIL deals go to disciplined athletes.

Financial Literacy 101: Budgeting, Saving & Spending

This may be the first time you've thought seriously about money. That's okay. Most schools don't teach this stuff—and that's exactly why this section matters.

Let's break down three basics:

1. **Budgeting**

A budget is a plan for your money. It tells you what's coming in and where it's going. Even if you're only working part-time, getting an allowance, or earning gift money, learning to manage that is key.

Start simple:

- How much money do I get each month?
- What are my basic needs (school supplies, meals, transportation)?
- What do I want to save for (gear, phone, college, clothes)?
- What can I spend without going broke?

Tracking your spending—even on a sticky note or notes app—is a game-changer.

2. **Saving**

Saving isn't just for adults. Start small, and build the habit early.

Tips:

- Open a savings account (with help from a parent or guardian)
- Save a portion of every dollar you get—try 10% to start
- Set specific goals like "save $100 for new cleats by spring season"

Saving gives you options. When NIL money starts flowing, you'll already know how to handle it wisely.

3. **Spending**

Smart spending is about value. Just because you *can* buy something doesn't mean you *should*.

Ask yourself:

- Do I really need this?
- Can I get it cheaper elsewhere?
- Is this going to help or hurt my long-term goals?

Athletes who learn this early avoid lifestyle inflation—the trap of spending just because they're earning.

Get Your Support Team Involved

You don't have to do this alone. In fact, you shouldn't. Your parents, guardians, coaches, and mentors are your first NIL advisors—even if they're learning along with you.

Freshman year is the time to start having money conversations at home:

- Ask your family about opening a savings account
- Talk about what happens when athletes earn income
- Learn how taxes work, even if you're not earning yet
- Discuss boundaries: if you start earning, how will that money be used?

Getting your family involved builds trust—and prevents future stress.

Learn Before You Earn

This might be the most important part of your freshman year when it comes to NIL: **Use this time to learn.** Don't rush into deals. Don't get caught up in hype. Don't assume you already know everything.

This is your year to:

- Study how NIL works across different states and school systems
- Watch what college athletes are doing right (and wrong)
- Read about taxes, contracts, and branding basics
- Think long-term: what do you want NIL to *do* for you?

The goal isn't just to get a deal. The goal is to get the *right* deal, at the *right* time, for the *right* reasons.

Freshman Year NIL Readiness Checklist

Here's a checklist to help you stay focused this year:

- I understand what NIL is and how it might affect me
- I've set 1–2 academic, athletic, and personal goals
- I've cleaned up my social media and started building a positive brand
- I track my spending weekly and save a percentage of my money
- I've talked with my family about money and NIL
- I've started learning about taxes and contracts
- I follow at least one NIL news source or athlete I admire
- I know who I can talk to if an NIL opportunity comes my way

Final Words for Freshman Year

Think of freshman year as your **off-season** when it comes to NIL. You're not expected to have all the answers or even to have income rolling in. But you *are* expected to prepare. This is your time to build a strong base before the pressure is on.

By the time your sophomore or junior year rolls around—and NIL becomes a real possibility—you'll already know how to manage your money, protect your brand, and make smart choices.

Starting early doesn't just make you smart. It makes you powerful.

Let's keep building.

Chapter 2: Clean Up Your Digital Footprint

Your Online Presence Is Part of Your Brand—Start Treating It That Way

You've probably heard the saying, *"The internet never forgets."* When it comes to your future as a student-athlete, especially in the NIL era, that phrase is more important than ever. Whether you realize it or not, **your digital footprint**—everything you've posted, liked, commented on, or been tagged in online—is part of how people see you.

And that includes college coaches, recruiters, media, and eventually, brands.

This chapter is about getting your online world right before the spotlight finds you. By the end, you'll know how to take control of your digital footprint, understand what to avoid, and start building a personal brand that aligns with your goals—without losing your personality.

Why Cleaning Up Your Digital Footprint Matters

As a freshman, you may not be thinking about NIL deals yet. You might still be adjusting to high school life and growing into your sport. But here's the reality:

- College recruiters start tracking athletes as early as 8th or 9th grade.
- Some high school athletes are already signing NIL deals by sophomore year.
- Brands, coaches, and media will Google you—before they even meet you.

The first impression you make may not be in person—it might be a search result.

Imagine this: A recruiter hears your name at a camp and searches you online. Your highlight reel pops up—great. Then they click your Instagram and see disrespectful comments, inappropriate memes, or careless language. In just a few seconds, they've made a judgment that might cost you an opportunity you never knew you had.

It's not about being perfect. It's about being intentional. You're building a reputation online every day—so it might as well work in your favor.

Social Media 101: Do's and Don'ts for Athletes

Social media can be a powerful tool for athletes. It's where you can:

- Share your progress
- Build a following
- Attract NIL deals
- Connect with teammates and fans
- Tell your story

But with great visibility comes great responsibility. Here's a basic breakdown to keep you on the right track:

Do:

- **Be authentic**: People connect with realness. Share your grind, your journey, and your passions.
- **Highlight others**: Celebrate your teammates, coaches, and community.
- **Use captions wisely**: Tell stories, not just stats.
- **Engage professionally**: Respond to comments in a positive way.
- **Stay coachable**: Post content that shows leadership, work ethic, and character.

Don't:

- Post inappropriate content (drugs, weapons, profanity, etc.)
- Share memes or music with offensive language
- Trash talk opponents, officials, or even your own teammates
- Get into arguments in comment sections or DMs
- Share every part of your personal life—privacy is power

Quick tip: If you wouldn't want your mom, your coach, or a future college to see it, don't post it. And don't just worry about your *posts*—pay attention to what you're tagged in, too.

Google Yourself: See What They See

Want to know what people see when they look you up? It's time to run a self-audit.

Here's how to do it:

1. **Open a private/incognito browser tab**
2. **Search your full name + city or team**
3. **Click through several pages**—not just the first one
4. **Check image results** too—old photos sometimes resurface

You might be surprised by what you find. Old posts. Team photos. A blog your school wrote. A post you were tagged in years ago.

This is what brands and coaches will see, too. Now ask:

- Does this reflect who I am today?
- Is there anything that needs to be taken down, hidden, or updated?
- Am I showing my character or just my stats?

If you find anything questionable:

- Delete it if it's your own
- Untag yourself if someone else posted it
- Ask a friend or parent to help if you're unsure

Start Creating a Basic Online Presence (Yes, Even as a Freshman)

Now that you've cleaned up the digital junk, it's time to start shaping your online image. Think of it like your locker—organized, personal, and a reflection of your values.

You don't have to be an influencer. You don't need thousands of followers. But you should start building a digital identity that reflects your goals.

What to include in your basic online presence:

- **A consistent profile name**: Use your real name or a variation (e.g., @_jordanreed)
- **A clean bio**: Include your sport, grad year, school, and goals
- Example: "Class of 2028 | RB @ East High | GPA: 3.7 | Faith • Family • Football"
- **Links to highlight videos or game film**
- **Pinned post or story highlights** with your best performances or community involvement

- **A good profile photo** (in uniform, smiling, or doing something positive)

Post content that reflects who you are—not just what you do:

- Training clips
- Game highlights
- Volunteering
- School events
- Interviews or news features
- Shoutouts to teammates or mentors

Even 1–2 solid posts a month can start to build your presence.

Start Shaping Your Personal Brand

Your personal brand is what people think of when they hear your name. It's your reputation—and it's built every day through your actions, your words, and your choices.

Here are a few questions to help define your brand:

- What do I want to be known for—on and off the field?
- What are three words I'd want people to use to describe me?
- Who are athletes I admire and why?
- What values do I want to show in everything I do?

This might sound deep, but it's important. Your brand could be:

- The quiet leader who lets actions speak
- The high-energy motivator
- The academic scholar-athlete
- The comeback story
- The community hero

- The consistent grinder

There's no right answer. Just make sure your brand is *real*—and that your online actions match it.

Tools and Tips to Manage Your Digital Presence

Here are a few practical tools and habits to keep your online game strong:

- **Social media check-ins**: Once a month, audit your posts and tags
- **Google Alerts**: Set up an alert for your name to get notified when new content pops up
- **Password protection**: Don't share your logins with teammates or friends
- **Private vs. public**: Consider keeping personal accounts private and having a public "athlete" profile
- **Create a media folder**: Keep your best photos, highlights, and news articles in one place for easy sharing

And remember, once NIL opportunities show up, brands will want a clean, easy-to-navigate online presence. Don't make them dig for it.

Freshman Year Digital Footprint Action Plan

Here's a step-by-step checklist to complete this chapter:

- Google yourself and document what you find
- Clean up your social media—delete old or inappropriate content
- Untag yourself from posts that don't align with your goals
- Update your bios with relevant info (name, sport, school, grad year)
- Choose a clean, professional-looking profile photo
- Post one piece of content that reflects your values or athletic journey
- Identify 3–5 athletes whose online presence you admire—and study

them
- Write down 3 words you want your personal brand to reflect
- Set a calendar reminder to do a monthly "digital audit"

Final Thoughts: Respect the Mirror You're Creating

The internet is a mirror you're building with every post, every like, and every tag. That mirror reflects your character, your hustle, and your potential. Colleges and companies will look at that mirror before they ever shake your hand. So don't wait until your junior or senior year to "clean things up."

Start now. Start small. And stay consistent.

What you post tells the world what matters to you. So make it count.

Chapter 3: Start the Conversations Early

Why Talking About Money, College, and NIL Starts Now—Not Later

You've probably been told to *"focus on school,"* or *"just keep playing hard and everything will fall into place."* And yes, putting in work on the field and in the classroom matters. But if you're serious about your future—especially in the NIL era—it's not enough to just grind. You also have to **talk**.

That's right. Conversations matter. Not just about your goals, but about money, expectations, and the kind of help you'll need along the way. Whether it's with your parents, your coaches, or your guidance counselor, starting early communication can help you avoid confusion, missed opportunities, and unnecessary stress later on.

You don't have to figure it all out right now, but the earlier you begin these conversations, the smoother your journey will be.

Talk With Your Parents or Guardians About Money, College, and Expectations

Your family might be your first team—and for a lot of student-athletes, they're also the people who will be most involved in your financial and college decisions. Even if you're not earning NIL income yet, it's still important to get on the same page.

Here's why it matters:

- **NIL decisions may involve your family's finances** (especially if they're managing your bank accounts or taxes)
- **Your college path may be shaped by scholarships, financial aid, and academic goals**
- **Clear expectations prevent miscommunication down the road**

Some families talk about money openly. Others don't. If your family hasn't had those conversations yet, now is the time to start. You don't need to have all the answers—just ask questions.

Try these conversation starters:

- "Have you heard about NIL for high school athletes? What do you think about it?"
- "If I started earning money, how would we handle it?"
- "Can we talk about how we're planning for college—are we saving anything or looking at scholarships?"
- "If I got a deal, who would help me review it?"
- "Can we make a plan together for what to do if an opportunity comes my way?"

These aren't always easy conversations, but they're necessary. They also show maturity—which can help your parents trust you with more responsibility down the road.

Bonus Tip:

If money has been a tough topic in your household, start small. Talk about saving for new cleats or managing your allowance. Over time, you can build up to bigger topics like taxes and NIL income.

Ask Your Coaches About NIL Awareness at Your School

Your coaches do more than just design plays and run practices—they often play a huge role in your development as a student-athlete. They may also be your first line of defense when NIL conversations start to swirl.

That's why it's smart to check in with your coaches early—*especially* in your freshman year—about where your school stands on NIL.

What to ask your coaches:

- "Is NIL allowed for athletes at our school or in our state?"
- "Do we have any rules about NIL opportunities or social media?"
- "If someone offered me a deal, who should I talk to first?"
- "Are there other athletes here who've done NIL deals before?"
- "Do you see this becoming more common while I'm in high school?"

These questions show leadership—and they give you insight into how much your school and staff are prepared for this new landscape. Some coaches will know the ins and outs. Others may still be learning. That's okay. The important thing is that you're starting the dialogue now.

Even if NIL isn't currently allowed in your state, the rules could change by next year. Being proactive means you'll be ready when that time comes.

Coach-Player Trust Tip:

Let your coaches know that you value their guidance and want to do things the right way. This builds trust and ensures they'll advocate for you when the time comes.

Connect With Your Guidance Counselor for College Planning

Your guidance counselor might not be on the sidelines, but they play a big role in your future. Counselors help students track academic requirements, understand scholarships and financial aid, and prepare for college admissions. As a student-athlete, it's especially important to get on their radar early.

Why meet with your counselor now:

- They can help you make sure your **GPA and class schedule meet NCAA eligibility requirements**
- They'll know which colleges offer academic and athletic scholarships
- They may have insights into **college prep programs, summer opportunities, or local NIL workshops**
- They'll keep you on track for *both* your athletic and academic goals

Things to discuss:

- "I'm a student-athlete, and I want to play at the next level. What do I need to do academically?"
- "Can you help me understand what classes or GPA I'll need to stay eligible?"
- "Do we have any NIL education resources or college planning tools I should use?"
- "What colleges should I start learning about based on my interests and grades?"

These meetings don't need to be long. Even a 10-minute check-in once per semester can help you stay on track. Plus, you're showing maturity and leadership by taking your future seriously.

Understand the Value of Surrounding Yourself With the Right Team

This is a big one. NIL—and life in general—isn't meant to be navigated alone. As you move through high school, the decisions will get bigger, the pressure will increase, and the stakes will rise. That's why you need a **team around you who will support your goals—not just your game.**

Think of it like building your own "dream team":

Role What They Can Help With

Parents/Guardians

Guidance, support, financial oversight

Coach

Development, character building, advocacy

Guidance Counselor

Academic planning, NCAA eligibility, scholarships

Mentor or Trusted Adult

Advice, big-picture thinking, life experience

Financial Educator or NIL-Aware Professional

Understanding contracts, budgeting, and taxes

These people won't all show up at once. Some will join your team naturally over time. Others you may have to seek out.

The key is to ask yourself:

- "Is this person giving me advice that protects my future?"
- "Are they in it for me—or in it for themselves?"
- "Do they challenge me to make better decisions?"

As NIL deals start becoming real, you'll find that people suddenly want to be part of your inner circle—sometimes for the wrong reasons. Building your core team now, while things are still quiet, helps you filter out noise later.

Building a Communication Game Plan

So how do you pull all this together? By creating a communication strategy. You don't have to be a perfect speaker, and you don't need fancy language. You just need to be *clear, consistent, and curious.*

Freshman Communication Checklist:

- Talk with your parents about money, goals, and expectations
- Meet with your guidance counselor at least once a semester
- Ask your coach about NIL awareness and team policies
- Identify one adult outside your family who you trust to give you solid advice
- Set boundaries early around who gets to weigh in on your NIL decisions (if/when they come)

Keep a notebook or notes app to track advice, questions, and helpful resources

This communication game plan will help you stay focused, supported, and informed—no matter what opportunities come your way.

Final Thoughts: Talk Now to Win Later

As a student-athlete, your schedule is probably packed. School, sports, workouts, maybe even a job or other commitments. It's easy to think, "I'll deal with that stuff later." But by *talking early*, you gain clarity, confidence, and a huge head start.

NIL is new, but conversations are timeless. The best athletes off the field are the ones who know how to ask questions, speak up, and lean on others when it counts.

Start your conversations now. You never know what doors they'll open.

Chapter 4: Financial Literacy 101

SOPHOMORE YEAR: Develop Your Game On and Off the Field

Sophomore year is when things start to click. You're no longer the new kid. You've got a year of experience under your belt, and people are beginning to notice. Coaches, teachers, teammates—and maybe even college recruiters or local businesses.

But while you're working on your jump shot, footwork, or 40-yard dash, you also need to be developing a skill that's just as important: **financial literacy**.

Money management isn't just something for grown-ups or athletes with NIL deals. It's a skill you build early, just like your game. And the truth is, **if you wait until money shows up to learn how to manage it, you're already behind**.

This chapter gives you the tools to start building a financial foundation now—so when the real checks come in, you're ready to handle them like a pro.

Create Your First Budget—Even If You Don't Have Income Yet

Let's start with the basics: **What is a budget?**

A budget is simply a **plan for your money**. It helps you:

- Know what's coming in
- Decide what's going out
- Stay in control (instead of feeling out of control)

Even if you're not earning from NIL yet, you probably have *some* money flowing through your life—maybe from:

- Allowance
- Birthday or holiday gifts
- A part-time job
- Cash for snacks, rides, or gear
- Helping out a neighbor or family friend

The *amount* doesn't matter. What matters is building the **habit** of tracking and planning your money.

Try This: The "Athlete's Budget Breakdown"

Let's say you get $50/month from various sources. Here's a sample budget:

Category/ % of Total /$Amount

Saving

20%

$10

Spending

60%

$30

Giving

10%

$5

Emergency Fund

10%

$5

You can adjust the categories, but this structure teaches you to:

- **Save consistently**
- **Spend with intention**
- **Be generous and responsible**

Track your spending for a week using a notes app, spreadsheet, or old-school notebook. Once you see where your money's going, it's easier to improve how you use it.

Open a Teen Checking and Savings Account (With a Parent or Guardian)

If you don't already have a bank account, now's the time. Having your own account (even one co-managed with a parent) gives you hands-on experience managing real money.

Benefits of opening a teen account:

- You learn how banks work
- You can set up direct deposit for jobs or NIL income later
- You get used to using debit cards responsibly
- You can start seeing your savings grow in real time

Most banks and credit unions offer **teen-friendly checking and savings accounts** that can be opened with a parent or guardian. These accounts usually:

- Have low or no monthly fees
- Come with a mobile app to track spending and balances
- Let parents monitor and transfer funds

When you open your account:

- Start by depositing birthday money, gift cards, or chore cash
- Use your **checking account** for daily spending
- Use your **savings account** to build toward bigger goals (gear, trips, even college)

Tip:

Ask your bank if they offer "round-up savings," where every purchase rounds up to the nearest dollar and saves the difference automatically. It adds up fast!

Learn the Basics of Credit and Debit Cards

At this stage, you've probably seen people using credit and debit cards without thinking much about the difference. But understanding how each one works is critical—especially if you want to avoid debt later.

Debit Card:

- Connected to your checking account
- Spends *your* money
- If the account is empty, your card usually gets declined
- Safer for beginners

Credit Card:

- Lets you **borrow** money from a bank or credit card company
- Comes with a **limit** (how much you can spend)
- You have to pay it back **with interest** if you don't pay in full each month
- Missing payments can hurt your **credit score**

So, when should you think about credit?

Probably **not** in your sophomore year. But this is the perfect time to learn how credit works.

Credit matters because:

- It affects whether you can buy a car or rent an apartment someday
- It can determine your interest rate on loans
- Some employers and landlords even check credit history

Ask your parents or guardians:

- How do credit scores work?
- Do we have a family credit card for emergencies?
- Can we look at a credit report together?

Just being aware of these things now will put you ahead of most of your peers—and even many adults.

Practice "Mock" NIL: What Would You Do With a $1,000 Deal?

Let's run a simulation.

Imagine you're offered $1,000 from a local business to promote them on Instagram and show up at a community event. You say yes (after reviewing the deal with a trusted adult). The check hits your account.

Now what?

You could:

- Spend it all on clothes or new sneakers
- Save it for college
- Give some to your family

- Put it into a long-term savings or investment account
- Reinvest in your own brand (new equipment, training, content)

Let's say you decide to break it down like this:

Category/Amount/Why

Savings

$300

Building your future

Spending (fun)

$200

Rewards and balance

Emergency Fund

$100

For unexpected costs

Reinvestment

$300

New cleats, video editor, logo design

Giving

$100

Donation to your youth league or school

This exercise isn't just hypothetical. It helps you **train your mindset** before the money ever comes in. That way, when the time comes, you won't be caught off guard or blow your first check out of excitement.

Money Mindset: Build Discipline Early

Being financially literate isn't just about math or numbers. It's about **discipline and decisions**.

Here's the truth: You don't rise to the level of your NIL income—you fall to the level of your financial habits.

That means:

- If you overspend with $50, you'll overspend with $5,000.
- If you save with $10, you'll save with $1,000.
- If you give with $5, you'll be generous when you have more.

That's why building these skills **before the deals come in** is key. You're training yourself just like you train for your sport—one rep at a time.

Sophomore Year Financial Literacy Action Plan

Here's a checklist to help you put this chapter into action:

- Track your spending for 1–2 weeks using a notes app or journal
- Create your first monthly budget—even with small amounts
- Open a checking and savings account with help from a parent or guardian
- Learn the difference between debit and credit cards
- Talk to your parents about how they handle money (credit, savings, bills)
- Practice a "mock" NIL deal and budget the $1,000
- Follow one financial YouTube channel, podcast, or TikTok for teens
- Write down one financial goal you want to reach by the end of the year

Final Thoughts: Start Small. Stay Consistent.

Sophomore year is when your game begins to evolve. You're getting stronger, smarter, and more confident on the field. But don't forget—*the same can be true with your finances.*

You don't need a paycheck to start building a financial playbook. All you need is the mindset to practice now so that when the money does come, you're ready—not reckless.

The best NIL athletes aren't just great at their sport—they're great at managing their money, time, and brand. And all of that starts with financial literacy.

You've got this. Let's keep building.

Chapter 5: Build Your Brand with Purpose

SOPHOMORE YEAR: Develop Your Game On and Off the Field

You don't have to be famous to have a brand.

You don't need a million followers to make an impact.

You don't have to wait until your senior year to start.

You already have a brand. The question is—are you building it with purpose?

In the NIL era, your name, image, and likeness are more than buzzwords. They're assets. They represent how people see you, what you stand for, and the value you bring beyond the scoreboard. This chapter is all about learning how to build and manage your personal brand in a way that's authentic, intentional, and ready for future opportunities.

Whether you're getting NIL deals now or just laying the foundation, you're already shaping your story—and this is your chance to take control of the narrative.

Why Branding Matters in the NIL Era

Let's be clear: NIL is about business. And business is built on **trust, visibility, and reputation**.

Your brand is your reputation—online and offline. It's what coaches, companies, and fans think of when they hear your name. Some athletes get NIL deals not just because they're good, but because they've built a positive, relatable, and consistent brand that aligns with what companies want.

The best part? You don't need to pretend to be something you're not. You just need to know who you are, and show it with consistency and purpose.

Create a Content Calendar: School, Sports, and Personality

You've got a lot going on—classes, practice, games, maybe a part-time job or clubs. So when it comes to building your brand, **consistency beats quantity**. You don't need to post every day, but you should aim to post with intention.

That's where a **content calendar** helps.

What is a content calendar?

It's a simple plan for what you're going to post, when you're going to post it, and why. It keeps your social media organized and aligned with your brand.

Here's a sample weekly breakdown for a sophomore student-athlete:

Day/ Post Type/ Example

Monday

Motivation

"Back to work. 6AM grind. Let's go. #MondayMindset" (with a workout clip)

Wednesday

School Life

"Study hall before practice. Gotta stay eligible. "

Friday
Game Day
Hype post with uniform photo or quote
Saturday
Highlight or Recap
Short video of a game moment or practice drill

Sunday
Personality
Share music, food, family time, or shoutouts to others

You don't have to post every day—just find a rhythm that works for you. Tools like Google Calendar, Notion, Trello, or even the Notes app can help you organize ideas.

Why it matters:

- It helps you stay consistent
- It prevents random, unprofessional posting
- It shows that you care about your image
- It attracts attention from recruiters and sponsors

Remember: **Content doesn't need to go viral—it just needs to be valuable.**

Identify Your Niche: What Makes You Unique?

There are thousands of student-athletes out there. So what makes you stand out?

Your **niche** is your unique combination of interests, personality, and story. It's the space you own—and the angle that makes your brand relatable and memorable.

Here are some ways to find your niche:

Ask yourself:

- What do I love besides my sport?
- What do people always come to me for?
- What challenges have I overcome that others can relate to?
- What values do I want to represent?

Common niche themes among student-athletes:

- **The Underdog Story** – Overcoming odds, coming from a small town, no offers yet but still grinding
- **Faith & Family** – Sharing your journey through your beliefs and personal values
- **Student First** – Focusing on academics, discipline, and leadership
- **Multi-sport or Multi-talented** – Playing multiple sports, or balancing sports and music, art, or entrepreneurship
- **Local Hero** – Deep community roots, mentoring youth, giving back
- **The Funny Athlete** – Using humor and personality to connect with followers

Your niche doesn't box you in—it gives you clarity. It tells the world: *"Here's what I'm about, and here's why I'm different."*

Once you know your niche, your content, captions, and partnerships all become more focused and aligned.

Engage With Your Community—Local Impact Matters

You don't need to be on ESPN to build your brand. In fact, some of the **most valuable NIL deals come from local businesses** who care about their community and want to support hometown athletes.

That's why engaging with your community is a powerful brand move.

Ways to get involved:

- Volunteer at youth sports clinics or summer camps
- Help with food drives, fundraisers, or community clean-up events
- Visit local elementary or middle schools as a guest speaker
- Support other school programs (band, cheer, drama, etc.)
- Give shoutouts to local businesses, mentors, or teachers

Not only does this feel good—it looks good. It shows that you're grounded, connected, and committed to more than just personal success.

Post about your involvement:

- "Great time helping with the youth flag football camp this weekend! Always cool to give back. "
- "Stopped by [local restaurant] today—thanks for the love and support! #SupportLocal"

This kind of engagement:

- Builds community loyalty
- Attracts local NIL opportunities
- Shows character and leadership
- Makes your brand authentic

Begin Capturing Photos and Videos to Build Your Story

If you wait until senior year to start documenting your journey, you'll miss out on all the growth along the way.

Start now.

You don't need fancy equipment—your phone is more than enough. But make it a habit to **capture the moments that show your hustle, progress, and personality**.

What to capture:

- Pre-game or post-practice clips
- Workout routines
- Study sessions or classroom wins
- Team moments (shout out teammates!)
- Family support—rides to practice, cheering at games
- Your "why"—motivational moments that show what drives you

These clips build your story. When you're ready to approach sponsors or schools, you'll have content that shows more than stats—it shows who you are.

Organize your content:

- Use folders on your phone or Google Drive
- Save content by month or category (Game Day, Workouts, Community)
- Use apps like CapCut, InShot, or Canva to make simple highlight reels

And always keep your best photos in one place for when opportunities come up.

Sophomore Year Brand Building Checklist

Define your brand values (what you want to be known for)

- Create a simple content calendar (even 2–3 posts per week)
- Clean up and update your bio across all platforms
- Start capturing content weekly—photos or videos
- Engage with your community through events or local support
- Identify your niche and focus your content to reflect it
- Follow 3 athletes who have a brand you admire—study their approach
- Shout out a local business or mentor in a post or story

- Ask for feedback from a coach or mentor on your public presence

Final Thoughts: Purpose Over Popularity

Your brand isn't about chasing clout. It's about consistency, connection, and character. Building a brand with purpose means every post, story, and interaction moves you closer to the person—and athlete—you want to become.

When NIL opportunities arrive, brands will look beyond your stats. They'll look at:

- How you show up online
- How you treat others
- Whether your values align with theirs

Sophomore year is the time to start building that brand—not with pressure, but with purpose. Do it your way. Stay real. Stay ready.

Chapter 6: Learn the Rules of the NIL Game

SOPHOMORE YEAR: Develop Your Game On and Off the Field

Why Understanding the Legal Side of NIL Is Just As Important as Landing a Deal

Imagine stepping onto the court for a championship game—but no one ever gave you the rulebook. You'd be lost, confused, or even penalized for something you didn't know was wrong.

That's exactly what happens when student-athletes enter the NIL space without understanding the rules. Just like any sport, **NIL has boundaries, policies, and regulations**—and if you don't learn them early, you could put your eligibility, reputation, or even financial future at risk.

This chapter is your playbook for staying on the right side of the rules—at your school, in your state, and beyond.

Understand Your State's High School NIL Laws (And How They Differ)

Here's the tricky part: **NIL laws for high school athletes are different in every state**. Some states allow NIL deals. Others ban them. And many are still trying to figure things out.

As of now, more than 30 state high school athletic associations have either approved, restricted, or are actively reviewing NIL opportunities for high school athletes.

What you need to know:

- Just because college athletes can earn from NIL **doesn't mean high school athletes can**—yet.
- Your eligibility to play could be affected if you break your state's rules.
- Rules change fast. A deal that's illegal today could become legal next semester.

How to find your state's rules:

- Visit your **State High School Athletic Association (SHSAA)** website
- Ask your **athletic director or coach** for the most current policy
- Use trusted NIL news sources (we'll share some below)
- Search: *"[Your State] High School NIL Rules 2025"* and confirm with an official source

State Examples (As of 2025):

State/ High School NIL Policy

California

NIL allowed for high school athletes

Texas

NIL banned for high school athletes

New York
NIL allowed with restrictions
Florida
Under review; pilot programs in some districts
Kansas
Currently prohibited, but policy being reviewed

Action Step: Write down your state's NIL status. If it's not allowed, when might it change? If it is allowed, what are the requirements?

Review the NCAA's Stance on NIL and Amateurism

Even though this book focuses on high school NIL, you still need to understand how the **NCAA sees NIL and amateurism**—because college is the next step for many student-athletes.

In 2021, the NCAA updated its policies to allow college athletes to earn NIL income **without losing eligibility**. This was a major shift.

But the NCAA still has guardrails. Here's what you need to know:

Key NCAA Guidelines:

- You can get paid for your **name, image, and likeness**, but not for performance (no pay-for-play)
- NIL deals **must not be used to recruit** athletes to a specific college
- You **must report NIL deals** to your school
- NIL income must be earned through **legitimate services** (social media posts, events, appearances, etc.)
- You can work with agents, lawyers, and advisors for NIL—**but not for professional contracts**

Why this matters in high school:

- Your NIL activity in high school could **impact your NCAA eligibility** if it violates state or school rules
- Some college coaches want to see how responsibly you handled NIL before recruiting you
- Understanding amateurism now will keep you out of trouble later

Pro Tip: NIL is legal, but not unregulated. Transparency, documentation, and ethical conduct still matter—at every level.

Know What You Can and Can't Do Under Your School's Rules

Even if your state allows NIL, your **school or school district may have its own policies**. That's why it's important to get clarity on what your school allows, encourages, or prohibits.

Questions to ask your coach, athletic director, or principal:

- Are student-athletes at this school allowed to participate in NIL deals?
- Can I wear my school jersey or use the school logo in sponsored content?
- Can I sign NIL deals during the school year or only during breaks?
- What do I need to report to the school (contracts, payments, posts)?
- Are there any restrictions around time, content, or companies I can work with?

Common school NIL restrictions:

- No use of school logos, uniforms, or facilities in NIL promotions
- No missing class or practice for paid appearances
- No deals with companies that conflict with school sponsors (e.g., if your school is a Nike school, you might not be able to promote Adidas)

Warning: Some NIL deals—even if they seem harmless—could violate school rules if you're not careful. Always get approval before signing or posting.

Begin Following NIL News, Updates, and Success Stories

NIL is a fast-moving game. Policies change. Trends shift. What worked six months ago might be outdated tomorrow.

That's why part of being NIL-ready is staying **informed**.

Here are a few ways to stay up to date:

Follow These NIL News Platforms:

- **On3 NIL**: College and high school NIL rankings, policy updates, athlete deals
- **Front Office Sports**: Sports business news, NIL trends
- **ESPN NIL Tracker**: Deal updates and athlete highlights
- **Opendorse**: NIL education platform for athletes
- **Your state's high school athletics site**

Use Social Media to Learn:

Follow college athletes, local athletes, and influencers in the NIL space. Watch what kind of deals they're signing, how they promote themselves, and how they stay within the rules.

Follow people who talk about:

- NIL education
- Athlete entrepreneurship
- Legal and financial NIL guidance
- Personal branding in sports

Find Role Models:

Pick 2–3 athletes you respect who are handling NIL well. Study their behavior. What kind of content are they posting? What are they saying about their partnerships? How are they balancing sports, school, and business?

Knowledge is power. The more you learn now, the less likely you are to make mistakes later.

Red Flags to Watch Out For

Knowing the rules also means recognizing when someone is trying to take advantage of you. Unfortunately, not everyone in the NIL space has good intentions.

Here are a few red flags:

- Pressuring you to sign quickly without reading the fine print
- Offering guaranteed money with little effort
- Asking for large upfront fees for representation
- Hiding terms or avoiding questions
- Saying "you don't need to tell your coach or parents"

If any deal, message, or offer feels off, trust your gut. Bring in a trusted adult, coach, or legal advisor before moving forward.

Sophomore NIL Rules Checklist

Research and write down your state's high school NIL status

- Ask your coach or athletic director about your school's specific NIL policies
- Read 1–2 articles about recent NIL deals or news in your area
- Identify 2 college athletes whose NIL approach you admire
- Create a "NIL Watchlist" of people, schools, or platforms to follow for

updates
- Write down 3 things you'd need to ask or confirm before signing any NIL deal
- Learn one new legal or financial NIL term this month (e.g., exclusivity clause, royalty, compliance)

Final Thoughts: Know the Rules, Play the Game the Right Way

Sophomore year is about development. And one of the smartest things you can do for your NIL future is to **study the rulebook while everyone else is still guessing**.

The athletes who win in the NIL space aren't just flashy—they're educated, prepared, and respectful of the game. That includes knowing what you're allowed to do, who you're allowed to work with, and how to keep your eligibility and reputation protected.

Build your NIL knowledge like you build your skills—one rep at a time.

Let's keep learning, let's keep leading, and let's keep building a future you can be proud of—on and off the field.

Chapter 7: Start Thinking Like a Business

JUNIOR YEAR: Position Yourself for Opportunity

Why Your Talent Is the Foundation—But Your Mindset Is the Multiplier

By your junior year, the stakes are higher. The spotlight is brighter. Scouts may be watching. College interest might be heating up. Maybe a local business has already reached out about working with you. Maybe you've had a taste of the exposure that comes with being *that* player.

But here's the truth that separates the successful from the almost-there:

At this level, it's not just about being an athlete anymore.

You have to start thinking—and operating—like a business.

Whether you're building your brand, negotiating a deal, managing your money, or presenting yourself to colleges and companies, everything you do sends a message about who you are and what you're worth.

This chapter will help you shift your mindset and behavior from *student-athlete* to *student-athlete-entrepreneur*. And no, you don't need to be making money yet. This is the year to prepare. Because when the opportunity shows up, you want to be the athlete who's ready—not the one who fumbles it.

Why Every Athlete Is Their Own Brand

Think about your favorite professional athlete. Chances are, they're not just known for how they play—they're known for *who they are.* That's branding.

Your **brand** is the total picture of your reputation—what people see, think, and feel when they hear your name.

In the NIL era, your brand can:

- Attract NIL deals
- Influence college recruiting decisions
- Open doors to internships, scholarships, and job opportunities
- Build a long-term platform beyond sports

But your brand doesn't build itself. It comes from the way you carry yourself—on and off the field.

Ask yourself:

- What do I want to be known for?
- What makes me different from every other athlete in my position or sport?
- What values do I show through my content, conversations, and choices?

Your brand doesn't need to be flashy. It just needs to be *consistent and authentic.*

Learn the Basics of Contracts, Taxes, and Marketing

By now, NIL opportunities may start to feel real. Whether you've been approached by a business or are simply planning ahead, you need to understand three things that come with every deal:

1. Contracts

A contract is a legally binding agreement. Before signing anything, you need to understand:

- **What's expected of you** (number of posts, appearances, deadlines)
- **What you're being paid** (flat fee, per post, free product)
- **How long the agreement lasts**
- **What happens if either party wants to cancel**
- **Exclusivity**: Does this deal prevent you from working with other brands?

Never sign a contract without reading it carefully and having a trusted adult, coach, or advisor review it.

2. Taxes

Yes, even as a student, you may owe taxes on NIL income. The money you earn from NIL is not a gift—it's business income. That means:

- You may need to **file a tax return**
- You might receive a **1099 form** from companies that pay you
- You should keep records of all NIL income and expenses
- In some cases, you may need to **pay quarterly taxes**

Start learning how taxes work now, even if you're not earning yet. It will save you stress—and money—later.

3. Marketing

Marketing is how you promote your brand to the world. For athletes, it includes:

- Social media presence
- Highlight videos and performance stats
- Community engagement
- Consistent messaging and tone
- Collaborating with other athletes or local businesses

Marketing is how people discover your story—and why they decide to work with you. Don't think of it as self-promotion. Think of it as storytelling.

Begin Tracking Your Performance and Engagement (On and Offline)

If you're serious about NIL, you need to know your numbers. That includes both your **athletic performance** and your **social media engagement**.

Track Your Athletic Stats:

- Game performance (points, assists, tackles, saves, etc.)
- Season averages
- Training benchmarks (speed, strength, skill development)
- Awards, honors, or rankings

Keep this in a Google Doc, spreadsheet, or notebook. When a coach or brand asks, you should be able to send a one-pager with your latest stats.

Track Your Social Media:

- Number of followers (Instagram, TikTok, YouTube, etc.)
- Average likes, comments, views
- Engagement rate (how active your followers are)
- What type of content gets the best response

Use tools like:

- Instagram Insights (built into the app)
- TikTok Analytics (requires a Creator or Business account)
- Third-party apps like Later, Hootsuite, or Buffer

The goal isn't to chase likes—it's to understand your **audience and influence**. Even if you have a small following, your value could be high if your followers are active and loyal.

Create a One-Page "Media Kit" About Yourself

A media kit is like a **resume for your brand**. It's a one-pager that introduces who you are, what you've accomplished, and why you'd be a great NIL partner.

What to include in your media kit:

- **Your name and contact info**
- **Sport, position, school, graduation year**
- **Short bio** (3–5 sentences)
- **Academic highlights** (GPA, test scores, honors)
- **Athletic achievements** (stats, awards, notable games)
- **Social media handles** + follower counts
- **Photos** (headshot + action shot)
- **Your brand identity** (values, niche, mission)
- **Any community involvement or volunteer work**
- **Fun facts or interests** (this helps companies connect with you)

Bonus: Include a quote from a coach or mentor that speaks to your character.

Keep your media kit updated every 2–3 months as your achievements, stats, and social following grow.

You can design your kit using:

- Canva (free and easy)

- Google Docs or Slides
- Adobe Express or PowerPoint

Once created, save it as a PDF. When someone asks, "Tell me about yourself," send the kit. You'll instantly look polished and professional.

Junior Year Business Mindset Checklist

Create a one-page athletic + brand resume/media kit

- Track your athletic and social media stats monthly
- Learn 5 basic contract terms (exclusivity, duration, deliverables, breach, compensation)
- Watch one video or read one article each week about NIL deals
- Follow 3 athletes or entrepreneurs you respect and study how they market themselves
- Begin drafting a financial log to track income and expenses (even if NIL hasn't started yet)
- Have a conversation with a trusted adult about how taxes work for self-employed income
- Practice explaining your brand or story in 30 seconds ("elevator pitch" style)

Final Thoughts: You're the Brand. The Business. The Boss.

You may not have a company logo. You may not be earning checks just yet. But the moment you step into the NIL world, **you become a business**—whether you realize it or not.

Junior year is the time to level up. Learn how to protect your time, present your brand, and manage your opportunities with purpose. The athletes who succeed long-term aren't just talented. They're disciplined. They're prepared. And they take their off-field business just as seriously as their on-field performance.

Don't wait to get "discovered."

Don't wait until your first deal to get organized.

Start thinking like a business now—so when the opportunity shows up, you already know how to close it.

Chapter 8: Build Your NIL Team

JUNIOR YEAR: Position Yourself for Opportunity

Because the Right People Can Make—or Break—Your Journey

You've heard it before in sports: *"It takes a team to win."* The same is true in NIL.

As you move deeper into your junior year, opportunities may start showing up in your DMs, inbox, or even in casual conversations. NIL has opened the door for student-athletes to become entrepreneurs, influencers, and community leaders—but it has also attracted people who want a cut of your potential.

This chapter is about building your **NIL team**—the circle of trusted people who can help you make smart decisions, protect your eligibility, and manage your growth the right way. Whether you've already been approached by someone offering to "represent" you or you're just preparing for the future, now's the time to get intentional about who's on your team—and who shouldn't be.

Who Should Be Part of Your Inner Circle?

When we say "NIL team," we don't just mean paid professionals. We're talking about your **support system**—the people who have your back, give you honest feedback, and want to see you succeed as a person, not just as an athlete.

Here's who should be in your core NIL team:

1. Family

Whether it's a parent, grandparent, aunt, uncle, or guardian, your family should be involved—especially in high school. They can:

- Help review opportunities and contracts
- Offer insight on values and long-term goals
- Protect you from being taken advantage of

2. Coach

Your coach knows your work ethic, leadership, and potential. They may also know what's happening with other athletes in your school or state. A great coach:

- Advocates for you in conversations with colleges or companies
- Keeps you focused when hype starts rising
- Reminds you that NIL isn't more important than your performance

3. Mentor

A mentor might be a former athlete, teacher, community leader, or family friend. Someone who's walked a similar path and can offer:

- Life wisdom
- Honest, unbiased advice
- A listening ear when things get confusing or stressful

4. Trusted Advisor (when appropriate)

This could be a financial advisor, attorney, or business manager—but only if they're **qualified, transparent, and trustworthy.** In high school, this role may be filled by your parents or a volunteer advisor from a nonprofit or school program.

You don't need to build this entire team overnight. But over time, you should be **intentional about who gets access to your NIL decisions.**

How to Evaluate Professionals (Agents, Advisors, and Reps)

At some point, someone may offer to "manage your deals," "grow your brand," or "get you paid." That sounds exciting—but it's where things can get dangerous fast.

Key roles you might encounter:

- **NIL Agent**: Helps negotiate deals and secure partnerships
- **Financial Advisor**: Manages money, investments, taxes
- **Marketing Rep**: Builds your brand and social presence
- **Lawyer**: Reviews contracts and protects your legal rights

Important note: In many states, high school athletes **cannot legally sign with agents.** Even in states where NIL is allowed, using a professional may be limited by school or state policy.

Before working with *any* professional, ask:

What licenses or certifications do you have?

They should be registered with appropriate state or national agencies. Look up their credentials.

Who else have you worked with?

Ask for references. If they can't name anyone or avoid the question, that's a red flag.

How are you paid?

Some get paid hourly. Some take a percentage. Others charge flat fees. Ask for everything in writing.

What's in the contract?

NEVER sign anything without reading and reviewing it with a parent, coach, or lawyer. Some reps will try to lock you in for multiple years. Be cautious.

Do I feel pressured or uncomfortable?

If someone is rushing you, talking down to you, or only focusing on money, that's a sign to step back.

Sample Questions to Ask Anyone Offering You Help

Use these questions when you're approached by someone who says they can help you with NIL. Write them down. Memorize them. Use them like a playbook.

1. "Can you explain what services you offer—and how you're qualified to offer them?"
2. "Have you worked with other high school or college athletes before?"
3. "How do you make money? Are there any upfront costs or fees?"
4. "Can I see a sample contract or agreement before committing?"
5. "What happens if I want to end our agreement?"
6. "Will you communicate directly with my parents and coach?"

7. "What's your plan to help me grow my brand—beyond just getting deals?"
8. "How do you make sure everything stays compliant with my school/state rules?"
9. "Can I have a few days to review and talk this over with my team?"

If someone avoids these questions or tries to make you feel guilty for asking them, walk away.

Practice Saying "No" and Identifying Red Flags

One of the most powerful things you can do as a young athlete is say "no" when something doesn't feel right.

It's your name. Your brand. Your future.

Here are some common NIL red flags to watch out for:

Red Flag / Why It's a Problem

"Don't worry about reading the contract."

You *should* read every contract. Always.

"You have to sign today or lose the deal."

Pressure tactics are manipulative.

"You don't need to tell your coach or parents."

Any legit professional will welcome your support team.

"I'll get you rich fast."

NIL is rarely instant money. Real deals take time.

"It's just a handshake deal—we don't need paperwork."

Verbal promises mean nothing without a contract.

Practice Saying:

- "Thanks for reaching out, but I need to run this by my parents and coach."
- "I appreciate the offer, but I'm not ready to make that kind of decision right now."

- "Can you send over something in writing for me to review?"
- "I'm not comfortable signing anything today. I'll get back to you after I talk to my team."

Saying "no" doesn't mean you're rude. It means you're in control.

Junior Year NIL Team Checklist

Identify who is currently in your support circle (family, coach, mentor)

- Choose 1–2 people to begin mentoring you through NIL decisions
- Write out your boundaries: who reviews NIL offers before you say yes
- Learn the roles of agents, advisors, and reps—and what they do
- Draft a list of 7–10 questions to ask any professional offering services
- Practice saying "no" with confidence in different situations
- Look up your state's rules around using agents as a high school athlete
- Make a list of NIL professionals you respect or follow—and study how they work

Final Thoughts: Protect Your Name Like It's a Championship

You've worked your whole life to build your name. Don't let someone mess it up with a shady deal, a rushed contract, or a promise they can't deliver.

Your NIL team isn't about hype—it's about wisdom.

The best athletes surround themselves with people who:

- Tell them the truth
- Keep them grounded
- Put their long-term future first

As NIL gets bigger, you'll hear louder voices offering "help." But don't let the volume distract you from what really matters. Your team—your *real* team—should always be built on trust, values, and vision.

Choose wisely. Ask questions. Protect your brand. You only get one name. Guard it like your jersey.

Chapter 9: Take Ownership of Your Story

JUNIOR YEAR: Position Yourself for Opportunity

Because If You Don't Tell Your Story, Someone Else Will

Every athlete has a story. Not just your stats or highlight reel—but who you are, what you've overcome, what you believe in, and how you treat others. That story becomes your brand. And your brand becomes your business.

Junior year is the season where potential starts turning into opportunity. Colleges are watching. Local businesses are listening. Your social media following may be growing. And it's time for you to lean in and start shaping the narrative—**on purpose.**

This chapter is all about owning your identity, refining your message, and making sure your reputation—online and offline—reflects your values, not just your performance. NIL success isn't just about how many followers you have. It's about the *trust* you build with your audience.

Write a Short Bio: Who You Are, What You Do, What You Stand For

Your bio is often the first thing a coach, brand, or fan sees when they check out your page. It's your digital handshake. A quick bio should answer three simple questions:

1. **Who are you?**
2. **What do you do?**
3. **What do you stand for?**

Think of it like a one-sentence mission statement for your life right now.

Examples:

- *"Class of 2026 | PG at Lincoln High | Faith. Hustle. Growth."*
- *"WR | 6'1 | 3.6 GPA | #TeamFirst mindset | Community over clout"*
- *"Soccer & STEM | Future engineer in cleats | Local leader & lifelong learner"*

Add this bio to your:

- Social media profiles (Instagram, TikTok, YouTube)
- Media kit
- Email signature (if reaching out to brands)
- Website or link-in-bio platform (like Linktree or Beacons)

And remember: your bio isn't set in stone. Update it each semester as your goals and story evolve.

Be Intentional With Every Post, Partnership, and Interaction

This is where ownership really comes into play. Every time you post, comment, repost, or tag someone—**you're communicating something about your brand**.

That doesn't mean you need to be fake or overly filtered. It means you should have a **purpose** behind what you share.

Post With Purpose:

- **Before you hit "Post"**, ask:
- *"Does this reflect who I am and where I'm going?"*
- *"Would a college coach or future partner be impressed or concerned by this?"*
- **Keep it real**, but keep it clean. You don't need to share every part of your life to be authentic.
- **Use your voice wisely.** If you're passionate about something (mental health, education, social justice, youth sports), speak up. Show the world you're more than a highlight machine.

Partnership Check:

If you get approached for an NIL deal—no matter how small—ask:

- "Does this brand align with my values?"
- "Would I use this product even if I wasn't paid?"
- "Will this help or hurt how people view me?"

Whether it's a local pizza place, a gym, or a clothing line, the companies you work with become part of your story. Choose carefully. And be proud of who you associate with.

Begin Reaching Out to Small Local Brands to Learn How Deals Work

You don't need to wait for deals to come to you. Junior year is the perfect time to practice.

Even if you're not ready to sign anything yet, you can start:

- Having conversations
- Building relationships
- Asking questions
- Learning how NIL works in the real world

Start local:

Reach out to small businesses in your town—places where you already shop, eat, or train.

Examples:

- Your favorite smoothie shop
- A local gym or trainer
- A family-owned restaurant
- A custom apparel shop
- A local photographer or videographer
- Youth camps or programs you've been part of

Sample message to a local business:

> Hi [Name], my name is [Your Name] and I'm a student-athlete at [Your High School]. I've followed your business for a while and really respect the work you're doing in our community. I'm learning about NIL and building my brand, and I'd love to connect, learn more about what it's like to work with athletes, and see if there's a way I can bring value to your business in the future—

even if it's just to understand how it works. Thanks for your time—looking forward to connecting!

The goal isn't always to land a deal. It's to **build a relationship**, practice professionalism, and learn how the process works. That experience will be just as valuable as a paycheck.

Use This Year to Build Trust and Grow Influence

Here's the part of NIL nobody talks about: **trust > followers.**

Brands don't just look for athletes with big numbers. They want athletes who:

- Communicate clearly
- Represent themselves well
- Inspire their audience
- Are consistent, not chaotic

If you only focus on looking cool or gaining followers, you might lose the one thing that actually matters: **your reputation**.

Ways to build trust:

- Respond to messages politely
- Stay humble in the wins, gracious in the losses
- Follow through on what you say you'll do
- Show appreciation to your supporters and community
- Avoid drama, gossip, or controversial online behavior

And most importantly: **just be a good human**. Kindness, respect, and character never go out of style.

Over time, this builds real influence—and real influence brings real opportunity.

Junior Year Ownership Checklist

Write or revise your short bio—who you are, what you stand for

- Update your social media profiles to reflect your values and story
- Audit your last 10 posts—do they reflect your brand or distract from it?
- Identify 3 local businesses you admire—follow and support them
- Draft a message to one small business asking to learn more about NIL
- Make a list of 5 things you want people to know about you beyond your sport
- Keep a log of conversations with brands, mentors, or advisors
- Commit to posting with purpose—less random, more intentional
- Begin thinking about what "influence" means to you (write it down)

Final Thoughts: Your Story Is Your Superpower

You don't have to be the top-ranked athlete or the loudest voice in the room to win in NIL. You just have to be **clear, consistent, and true to your story**.

Junior year is a window of time where you get to shape your narrative before the spotlight is fully on. That's a gift. Use it wisely. Learn the craft. Build your voice. Connect with people who care about your growth—not just your numbers.

Because at the end of the day, NIL isn't just about deals. It's about **developing the discipline to lead yourself—and inspire others—in everything you do.**

Own your story now, and it will take you further than any brand ever could.

Chapter 10: Taxes, Payments, and Financial Basics

JUNIOR YEAR: Position Yourself for Opportunity

B*ecause Making Money Is One Thing—Managing It Is Another*

NIL means you can finally earn money from your name, image, and likeness. That's a big win for athletes. But what a lot of people don't tell you is this:

As soon as you start earning, you're also running a small business.

That means you're responsible for understanding things like taxes, payments, record-keeping, and savings—even while you're still in high school.

This chapter isn't here to scare you. It's here to empower you. If you understand the basics, you'll be in a great position to not just make money—but to keep it, grow it, and protect your future.

Let's break it down in a way that's simple, smart, and action-oriented.

What Taxes You'll Owe—and When

Here's the hard truth: **The money you earn from NIL is not tax-free.**

When you get paid for a brand deal, a camp appearance, a social media post, or any other NIL activity, that money is considered **self-employment income** by the IRS. And yes—even if you're in high school—you may owe taxes on it.

What does this mean?

If you earn:

- **Over $400/year** from NIL, you may need to pay **self-employment tax**
- **Over the IRS standard deduction** (currently around $13,850 as of 2025), you'll also owe **federal income tax**
- Some states also have **state income tax** you may need to pay

You're now what the IRS considers a "**sole proprietor.**" That's just a fancy way of saying: "You're in business for yourself."

When are taxes due?

Most students will file taxes **once a year**, usually by **April 15th**.

BUT—if you're earning consistently throughout the year, especially large amounts—you may be required to make **quarterly tax payments**.

Pro tip:

Even if you only make a few hundred dollars, start tracking and preparing like you're making thousands. Why? Because that mindset helps you avoid mistakes when things scale up.

Keeping Receipts, Logs, and Paperwork Organized

Good records are your financial playbook. Without them, you can't:

- File accurate taxes
- Prove your income or expenses

- Track your growth
- Apply for scholarships, grants, or college programs that ask about your finances

What should you keep?

Type/ Examples

Income Records

Payment confirmations, 1099 forms, PayPal/Venmo deposits, brand contracts

Expenses

Gear, travel, content tools, phone/data plan, photographer fees

Receipts

Physical or emailed—save every one

Mileage Logs

If you drive to a paid event or shoot, track the miles

Invoices

If you send one for your work, keep a copy

Emails and DMs

Any business conversation—save a screenshot or PDF

Bank Statements

Track what goes in and out of your NIL account

Tools that help:

- Google Drive or Dropbox folder: Create folders by year or project
- A "NIL Notebook" or Google Sheet for tracking payments
- Apps like **Expensify**, **QuickBooks Self-Employed**, or **Wave** (free)
- Even your phone's Notes app works—just start somewhere

The key is to **stay organized from Day 1**. Don't wait until tax season to dig through texts and emails.

Hire Help or DIY? (Bookkeeper, CPA, or Parent With Guidance)

You don't have to do this alone—but you *do* have to be involved. Whether you manage your money with a spreadsheet, a parent, or a pro, the goal is to build financial awareness early.

Who can help?

- **CPA (Certified Public Accountant):** They can help you file taxes, understand what you owe, and avoid costly mistakes.
- **Bookkeeper:** Helps track income/expenses but doesn't usually offer tax filing services.
- **Parent/Guardian:** With guidance from an advisor or online resources, they can help you get started.
- **Trusted Advisor/Coach/Mentor:** Can recommend professionals or resources for support.

When to hire a professional:

- You've earned **over $1,000–$2,000 from NIL** and expect to keep earning
- You've received a **1099 tax form**
- You have **multiple NIL partnerships**
- You want help setting up a **business structure** or planning for college/retirement

Tip:

Even if you hire help, **you're still the CEO.** Learn what's happening with your money. Ask questions. Stay involved.

Smart Saving Strategies for College and Beyond

Here's a common NIL mistake: an athlete gets paid—and spends every dollar.

Here's a better move: treat every paycheck like a chance to build the future.

The 50-30-20 Rule (Simplified for NIL):

- **50% = Save** (put away for college, emergencies, or investment)
- **30% = Spend** (enjoy your money—within reason)
- **20% = Give or Grow** (donate, invest, or reinvest in your brand)

If you make $1,000 from a local deal, it could break down like this:

- $500 to savings
- $300 for fun or personal use
- $200 to give back to your community or grow your brand (buy gear, hire a videographer, etc.)

Open These Accounts:

- **Teen Checking Account**: For everyday spending and deposits
- **Teen Savings Account**: For emergency fund or goals
- **529 College Savings Plan**: Ask your parents about contributing here
- **Roth IRA** (if you have earned income): Start investing early with the help of a parent or financial advisor

Why it matters:

The money you save now could help you:

- Buy a car

- Pay for college
- Invest in your future business
- Create options when your playing days end

Money = freedom. And freedom comes from **discipline and planning.**

Junior Year NIL Finance Checklist

Create a Google Sheet or notebook to track income and expenses

- Talk to a parent/guardian about filing taxes and saving receipts
- Open a checking and savings account (if you haven't already)
- Learn what a 1099 form is and what it means
- Start organizing receipts, contracts, and agreements digitally
- Meet with a CPA, teacher, or trusted adult to ask about tax basics
- Make a plan for saving a % of your next NIL payment
- Download a budgeting app or use a spreadsheet to track where your money goes
- Watch 1–2 YouTube videos about NIL taxes or self-employment income
- Write down one money goal (college, gear, investment, donation, etc.)

Final Thoughts: Manage the Money Before It Manages You

It's easy to get excited about earning money through NIL. And you should be. You've earned it. But your money is only powerful if you know what to do with it.

When you understand taxes, plan your savings, and track your business, **you go from just making money—to building wealth**.

You don't need to be perfect. You just need to be present, prepared, and proactive. Start small. Stay consistent. Ask questions. And remember:

You are not just an athlete. You are the CEO of your brand.

And now, you've got the tools to lead it well.

Chapter 11: Peer Pressure and Lifestyle Creep

How to protect your wallet—and your peace—when everyone's watching.

So, you just signed your first NIL deal. Maybe it's $500. Maybe it's a few thousand. Maybe it's free gear, smoothies, or a social media promo that gets hundreds of likes. Either way, **people are watching.**

Friends start texting you more.

People you barely know start calling you "famous."

Teammates start asking for rides.

Strangers start assuming you've "got it like that."

And suddenly, the pressure is real—not just to perform, but to **provide**, **post**, and **prove**.

Welcome to the side of NIL nobody talks about enough:

Peer pressure and lifestyle creep.

This chapter is about what happens after the check clears—when the temptation to "flex" is just as strong as the urge to save. When your circle starts treating you differently. And when staying true to your values becomes the biggest win of all.

When Friends Start Asking for Money or Freebies

Let's get one thing straight: **having NIL money does not make you everyone's ATM.**

Whether you earn $500 or $5,000, it's **your responsibility**—not your obligation to fund someone else's snacks, shoes, or Uber ride.

But here's what might happen:

- A friend asks you to buy them food "just this once."
- A teammate jokes, "Man, you're rich now. Hook me up!"
- Someone asks if they can borrow your gear or use your discount code.
- You start to feel like saying no makes you selfish.

What to Do:

1. **Set clear boundaries early.**
2. You don't owe anyone an explanation. Try:

"I'm on a budget and trying to be smart with what I earn."
"I've got goals I'm saving for, so I'm keeping my spending tight."

1. **Practice polite but firm responses.**

"I can't do that right now, but I appreciate you asking."
"I'm sticking to a plan—I hope you understand."

1. **Have someone in your corner.**
2. A parent, mentor, or coach who can help you stay firm when pressure builds.

Reminder: Real friends won't expect you to prove your loyalty with money.

The Pressure to "Flex" Online

You scroll Instagram.

Your teammate just bought new shoes.

Another athlete you follow is rocking designer clothes.

A local influencer posts a video with a new chain and says, "Just copped this with my NIL bag ."

And now you're thinking: *"Should I be doing more?"*

This is how the pressure starts.

Even if you didn't plan to overspend, the urge to show that you've "made it" can sneak up on you. And in the NIL world, **your image can feel like your income**—so it's easy to confuse branding with bragging.

Reality Check:

- Posting every purchase isn't proof of success.
- Not everyone showing off money actually has it.
- Some people flex online but are broke in real life.
- Likes don't equal legacy.

How to Protect Your Image Without Overspending:

- Show your values, not just your valuables.
- Post content that tells your story: workouts, community work, behind-the-scenes moments.
- Use your influence to inspire, not impress.
- Avoid the trap of "buying things just to post them."

Recognizing Lifestyle Inflation

Lifestyle inflation means this: the more you earn, the more you start spending—**without realizing it.**

It starts small:

- You upgrade from fast food to high-end takeout every night.
- You switch from $60 shoes to $200 designer sneakers.
- You start covering group bills to avoid awkwardness.
- You buy a new phone—not because you need it, but because others have it.

Before you know it, your NIL check is gone—and you're wondering why you're still broke.

How to Spot Lifestyle Creep:

- You feel pressure to "keep up" with what others are doing or wearing.
- You start spending more than you save—even if your income increased.
- Your wants start to feel like needs.
- You feel guilty or embarrassed saying no to a purchase.

How to Stop It:

1. **Stick to your budget—even when the money increases.**
2. Just because your income grows doesn't mean your lifestyle should.
3. **Make upgrades based on needs, not feelings.**
4. Don't let emotions lead your wallet.
5. **Save before you spend.**
6. Set automatic savings goals for college, emergencies, or business growth.
7. **Celebrate wins differently.**
8. Reward yourself with experiences, rest, or time—not just things.

Staying Grounded in Your Values

When NIL attention starts coming in, so do distractions. You may feel pulled in different directions:

- Trying to make everyone happy
- Saying yes to deals that don't align
- Posting content that gets clicks but doesn't reflect who you are
- Feeling fake, even if you're "winning" online

But the best thing you can do with your NIL opportunity?

Stay grounded.

Ask Yourself:

- What do I want to be known for?
- Does this deal or decision align with my purpose?
- Would I still do this if no one saw it on social media?
- Will this help me grow—or just get me attention?

Anchoring Practices:

- Write down your top 3 values (examples: faith, family, discipline, purpose)
- Revisit your goals monthly—financial, academic, athletic
- Have a "check-in circle" of 1–2 trusted adults who can keep you focused
- Take intentional breaks from comparison and content

> ***Reminder:*** *You are not what you wear.*
> *You are not how many followers you have.*
> *You are not your latest deal.*

You are your **decisions**, your **discipline**, and your **direction**.

Quick NIL Self-Audit: Peer Pressure & Lifestyle Creep Edition

- Do I feel like I have to spend money to "keep up"?
- Have I ever bought something just to post it online?
- Have I said "yes" to something that didn't align with my values?
- Have I shared a post I didn't fully believe in, just for money or likes?
- Have I loaned money to someone that made me uncomfortable?
- Have I spent more since my first NIL deal—even on things I don't need?
- Do I feel anxious when I say "no" to a friend asking for help or cash?
- Do I know how to explain my budget and boundaries to my circle?

If you answered "yes" to 3 or more, it's time to reset your mindset. That's not failure—it's awareness.

Final Word: Keep Your Power

Peer pressure is real. Lifestyle creep is sneaky. NIL brings freedom—but also responsibility.

Here's what you have to remember:

- You earned this opportunity. You get to decide what to do with it.
- You don't owe anyone access to your money, brand, or influence.
- You don't need to flex for anyone who doesn't contribute to your growth.
- You have the power to say "no"—and that's one of the most professional things you can do.

Keep your focus. Keep your values. Keep your future in mind.

Because when the moment passes and the money's gone, what matters most is what you built—and who you became.

And that's a kind of wealth that can't be faked, flexed, or inflated.

Chapter 12: Final Checklist Before Graduation

SENIOR YEAR: Prepare for the Next Level

Because Readiness Isn't Just About Your Game—It's About Your Growth

You've made it to senior year. You've competed, grown, posted, planned, and maybe even profited. Whether you've signed an NIL deal, received college offers, or simply grown more confident in who you are, this journey has been about way more than sports—it's been about life.

But before you walk across that stage, sign your letter of intent, or move into your dorm, it's time to pause and ask: **Am I ready for what's next?**

Not just ready to play. Ready to **handle NIL opportunities. To manage money. To protect your name. And to walk into adulthood with the confidence that you've got a foundation others wish they had.**

This chapter is your final walkthrough—a checklist to help you evaluate, tighten up, and step into your future with clarity and purpose.

Is Your Brand College-Ready?

By now, you know your brand is more than a logo or highlight reel. It's your reputation. The way you post, speak, and show up in real life matters just as much as how you perform on game day.

Ask Yourself:

- Do my social media profiles reflect who I am and what I stand for?
- Is my bio up to date with my graduation year, sport, and college (if committed)?
- Are there any posts I need to clean up or remove?
- Do I highlight leadership, character, and consistency—not just hype?
- Have I started building a brand that's bigger than my stats?

Why it matters:

Colleges are watching. So are brands. But more importantly, **you're setting the tone for who you'll be when nobody's looking.**

Your digital presence should say:

- "I'm focused."
- "I know who I am."
- "I take this seriously."

If it doesn't, now's the time to fix it—before your freshman year of college becomes your first NIL headline.

Do You Have a Basic Financial Literacy Foundation?

You don't need to be a CPA to succeed—but you do need to understand the basics.

Can you confidently say:

- I know the difference between a checking and savings account
- I've created and followed a budget
- I understand what taxes I may owe on NIL income
- I know what a 1099 form is and why it matters

- I've started saving for college, emergencies, or future goals
- I can explain what a credit score is and how to protect it
- I understand how to evaluate whether a deal or purchase is worth it

If not, revisit earlier chapters or find someone to help guide you. **You can't afford to be financially unprepared—especially with money and opportunity coming your way.**

Have You Communicated with Your Future College About NIL?

If you've committed to a college, it's time to talk about NIL—**before you show up on campus.**

Each college handles NIL differently. Some schools offer full NIL support with marketing teams, advisors, and brand connections. Others provide little to no support. Knowing what to expect helps you plan ahead and avoid surprises.

Questions to ask your college coach or compliance officer:

- "What are the school's policies on NIL?"
- "Do I need to report NIL deals to the compliance office?"
- "Can I use school facilities, logos, or uniforms in my content?"
- "Does the school have any partnerships or NIL education programs?"
- "Are there preferred professionals (agents, accountants, advisors) I can work with?"

Why this matters:

Even though the NCAA allows NIL, **you're still responsible for following school-specific rules.** Missteps could hurt your eligibility or relationship with your team.

Make communication a habit. Don't assume. **Ask. Clarify. Document.**

That's how professionals operate.

Are You Mentally Prepared for Money, Pressure, and Opportunity?

Let's keep it real: NIL brings more than income. It brings exposure, expectation, and sometimes, stress.

You may face:

- People treating you differently because of your deals
- Pressure to keep up with other athletes' success
- Temptations to spend money quickly
- Unwanted opinions from social media or even your peers
- The challenge of balancing sports, academics, and business

That's why mental preparation is key. You've built the tools throughout this book. Now it's time to check your mindset.

Reflect:

- Do I know who I am *without* NIL?
- Can I handle criticism, pressure, or attention without losing focus?
- Do I have a support system I trust—family, coach, mentor, counselor?
- Do I know how to set boundaries with people who want something from me?
- Am I more focused on building my future than impressing people?

Protect your peace. Guard your energy. Prioritize your health. No deal is worth your identity, joy, or mental clarity.

Senior Year Final NIL Readiness Checklist

Here's a full checklist to complete before graduation:

- My social media profiles are clean, current, and aligned with my values
- I have a clear, written bio and personal brand identity
- I've created a one-page media kit or NIL resume
- I understand how NIL income is taxed and how to track it
- I've opened a checking and savings account (and started budgeting)
- I've identified trusted adults or professionals to help with deals and finances
- I've talked to my future college about NIL policies and expectations
- I've practiced saying "no" and spotting red flags
- I've started saving for future goals—not just spending for now
- I've taken time to reflect on who I am, what I want, and how I want to lead

Final Thoughts: NIL Is a Privilege—So Use It With Purpose

Graduation marks the end of one journey—and the beginning of another. You've grown as an athlete, but more importantly, you've grown as a person. NIL isn't the finish line. It's just one tool in a much bigger story you're writing.

So use it wisely.

Treat your name like it matters—because it does.

Build for long-term impact—not short-term attention.

And walk into your next chapter knowing that you're more than ready.

You've got the mindset. You've got the playbook. Now go make the most of it.

Chapter 13: Entrepreneurship for Student-Athletes

Using your NIL to build something bigger than yourself.

You've probably heard people say:

"NIL is more than just getting paid—it's a chance to build a business."

But what does that actually mean? What does it look like for a high school athlete to *become an entrepreneur*? How do you go from promoting someone else's brand to *creating your own*?

This chapter will walk you through what entrepreneurship means, how to get started, and how your NIL identity can open doors not just for deals—but for ownership.

Turning NIL Into a Business

Most student-athletes start with NIL by promoting **other people's businesses**—which is great. But you can also create your own.

Examples of Athlete-Owned NIL Businesses:

1. **Merchandise (Merch)**

- Create your own brand with custom hoodies, shirts, wristbands, or stickers.
- Use catchphrases, slogans, or personal logos.
- Sell online through platforms like Shopify, Etsy, or Printful.
- Market through your social media with behind-the-scenes content.

2. **Training Camps / Clinics**

- Host sports clinics or skills camps for younger athletes.
- Offer one-on-one training sessions in your sport.
- Partner with local gyms or schools for space.
- Charge a small fee and provide a high-value experience.

3. **Digital Products**

- Sell playbooks, workout plans, or nutrition guides you use.
- Offer digital training videos, drill demos, or mindset tips.
- Create an eBook or course about your athletic journey.

4. **Content Creation**

- Start a YouTube channel, podcast, or blog about your sport and NIL experience.
- Share your journey, training tips, or athlete lifestyle content.
- Monetize through ads, sponsorships, or affiliate links.

Key Takeaway: *If people are watching, following, or learning from you—you have a business opportunity waiting to be built.*

LLCs and Business Accounts: When and How to Set Them Up

If you're earning NIL money or running a small business, it's time to get organized like one.

What is an LLC?

An **LLC (Limited Liability Company)** is a legal business structure that separates your personal finances from your business activities.

Why consider starting one?

- Adds **legitimacy** to your brand.
- Helps with **tax reporting** and business deductions.
- Provides **legal protection** if something goes wrong.
- Makes it easier to **open a business bank account** and get paid.

When to Set It Up:

- If you're earning more than $1,000 consistently.
- If you're selling products or offering paid services.
- If you're entering into long-term NIL deals or partnerships.

How to Set It Up:

1. **Choose a name** (Example: JC Training & Apparel, Jalen Carter Athletics LLC).
2. **Register your LLC** with your state (varies by state, usually online through the Secretary of State).
3. **Get an EIN** (Employer Identification Number) from the IRS—it's like a Social Security number for your business.
4. **Open a business checking account** to keep your NIL income and expenses separate from personal money.

Tip: Do this with your parent or guardian if you're under 18. They can help you register and act as the legal representative.

Using Your Brand to Launch a Business Beyond Athletics

Your playing days won't last forever. But your brand—and your ability to create value—can.

Think Bigger Than NIL Deals:

- NIL is a platform, not a paycheck.
- What are you passionate about?
- What do people come to you for?
- What skills are you learning as an athlete that can transfer into business?

Real-Life Examples:

- A high school quarterback starts a podcast about leadership and teamwork.
- A track star launches a mental health brand to help teen athletes cope with anxiety.
- A basketball player creates an online store for custom socks and accessories.

How to Turn Your NIL Brand into a Launchpad:

1. **Identify your niche.** What are you known for? What do you care about? What value can you give others?
2. **Build an audience around your story.** Share your training, behind-the-scenes, and personal insights—not just highlights.
3. **Create a simple product or service.** Keep it real, useful, and authentic.
4. **Test, learn, and improve.** Start small, track feedback, and grow

slowly.

Being an entrepreneur is about solving problems, creating value, and serving people—not just selling things.

Lessons from Other Teen Entrepreneurs

Let's look at some real-world stories of young athletes and entrepreneurs who used their talent, voice, and NIL platform to build something lasting:

Mikey Williams (Basketball)

One of the first high school athletes to sign major NIL deals, Mikey has also worked on building his brand through merchandise, partnerships, and media. He's not just cashing checks—he's building a lifestyle brand around his personality.

Haley and Hanna Cavinder (Basketball)

The twin athletes used their TikTok following to build a strong digital presence. With NIL, they signed deals but also leveraged their brand to create long-term partnerships and explore media careers beyond basketball.

Jasmine Green (Track & Field, Fictional Example)

Created a virtual coaching platform for young female runners in under-represented communities. She recorded sprint workouts, form tips, and Q&As, all hosted on Instagram and YouTube. She earned sponsorships and inspired the next generation.

Marcus Lee (Football, Fictional Example)

Started "Humble Hustle," a lifestyle brand that promotes hard work and self-discipline. Began with hats and hoodies sold through Shopify. Now runs his own camp, podcast, and blog teaching younger athletes about mindset.

Entrepreneurship Starter Checklist for Student-Athletes

Identify your business idea: merch, training, content, or services

- Choose a name for your business or brand
- Check your state's NIL and business laws (ask a mentor or advisor)
- Create a separate bank account or payment platform (Venmo Business, PayPal)
- Draft a simple business plan (what you'll offer, to whom, and how you'll market it)
- Set up an LLC if your business grows or earns consistently
- Track all income and expenses (use a spreadsheet or budgeting app)
- Build your brand: content calendar, colors, voice, values
- Ask for feedback from a trusted adult or mentor
- Reinvest a portion of your profits into growth (ads, gear, coaching)

Final Word: You're Not Just the Brand—You're the CEO

Entrepreneurship is more than a hustle—it's a mindset.

It's about believing in your ability to create, lead, serve, and earn—without waiting for permission.

So whether you're launching a clothing line, hosting your first camp, or just learning how to manage a budget and a brand, remember this:

- NIL is your opportunity.
- Entrepreneurship is your ownership.
- And **your name is the business—so build it like it matters.**

You don't have to wait to be older, richer, or more "established."

You just have to start smart, stay consistent, and **be willing to grow.**

Athletes don't just play anymore—they build.

And you've got everything you need to do just that.

Chapter 14: Understanding College Recruiting and NIL

Why your future is about more than the scholarship offer—or the NIL deal.

For generations, the college recruiting process focused on two questions:

1. Who's offering me a scholarship?
2. Where can I get playing time?

Today, there's a third—and equally important—question to add:

What are this school's NIL opportunities and support like?

The rise of NIL has changed the game for college recruiting. Some schools are creating entire ecosystems around NIL—complete with brand-building programs, collectives, media training, and even social media strategy. Others are still figuring it out.

So what does this mean for you as a high school athlete? It means you need to show up not just as a prospect—but as a **prepared, brand-aware, and values-driven student-athlete** who understands the full picture.

This chapter will help you ask the right questions, avoid the wrong assumptions, and choose the school that fits you—not just your wallet.

How Your NIL Readiness Affects Your Recruitment

College coaches are watching more than your highlight tape. They're also paying attention to:

- How you handle attention
- Your social media presence
- Your leadership and maturity
- Your understanding of NIL—and your responsibility within it

In other words, **you are now both an athlete and a brand**. And the more prepared you are for that reality, the more attractive you become to the right program.

What NIL Readiness Looks Like:

- You know how NIL works in high school and college
- You have a clean, intentional social media presence
- You understand the basics of contracts, taxes, and professionalism
- You've already worked with a local brand or created content consistently
- You treat your name and image like it matters—because it does

Coaches and college NIL staff want players who are coachable, smart, and ready to handle the pressure that comes with opportunity. Your NIL readiness signals that you're not just a great player—you're a future leader.

Questions to Ask on Campus Visits About NIL Support

When you go on an official or unofficial college visit, you're evaluating more than just facilities and locker rooms. You're evaluating your future.

If NIL is important to you—and it should be—**you need to treat it like part of your recruiting criteria.**

Here are some smart, respectful, and insightful questions to ask during your campus tour or recruiting conversations:

For Coaches:

- "How does your program support athletes with NIL education?"
- "Are there any restrictions here on what kinds of deals we can do?"
- "Are players allowed to work with agents or reps during college?"
- "How do you make sure NIL doesn't become a distraction for your team?"
- "Do you involve families in NIL decisions during the recruiting process?"

For NIL or Compliance Staff:

- "What is your school's NIL reporting process?"
- "Are there on-campus resources to help with taxes, legal, or brand management?"
- "Does your school offer workshops or training on content creation and business skills?"
- "Do you provide access to local or national brands through partnerships or marketplaces?"
- "Can you show me examples of other athletes on campus successfully navigating NIL?"

For Current Student-Athletes (if you get the chance):

- "How supported do you feel here with NIL?"
- "Is the NIL talk real—or just part of the pitch?"
- "How do you balance academics, athletics, and NIL demands?"

Write these questions down. Bring them with you. A school that avoids or brushes off NIL conversations may not be ready to support your long-term success.

Reviewing the School's NIL Collectives and Brand-Building Programs

What's a Collective?

An **NIL collective** is an organization—usually not officially part of the athletic department—that helps student-athletes monetize their NIL through coordinated deals, partnerships, or fan contributions.

Some collectives:

- Arrange deals with local businesses
- Pay athletes for appearances, promotions, or community work
- Offer training in financial literacy, business, or marketing
- Focus on specific sports (like football or basketball)

Tip: Some collectives have better reputations than others. Do your research.

What to Look For:

- Is the collective organized and transparent?
- Are athletes required to do something in return for money (appearances, content, etc.)?
- Are deals managed legally, with contracts and tax help?
- Does it support all athletes—or just the biggest stars?

Brand-Building Support on Campus

Some colleges now offer:

- **Personal brand coaching**
- **Social media workshops**
- **Access to videographers or content creators**
- **Connections to brands, alumni, and media outlets**

- **Career readiness programs for life after sports**

If a school is investing in these things, it shows they care about your future—not just your stats.

Choosing a School That Fits You—Not Just One Chasing a Bag

You will hear stories of athletes picking schools based on NIL offers alone.

But let's be honest: **If the NIL money is the main reason you choose a school, you may be setting yourself up for regret.**

Here's why:

- NIL deals can disappear faster than they arrive.
- If you're unhappy with the coaching, academics, or team culture, it won't matter how much money you make.
- Transferring schools isn't always easy or fun.
- Long-term fit leads to long-term success—on the field, in the classroom, and beyond.

Ask Yourself:

- "If this school offered no NIL support, would I still want to be here?"
- "Can I see myself growing here as a person—not just an athlete?"
- "Is the program truly invested in who I am, or just what I can do?"
- "Will I be surrounded by the right mentors, professors, and teammates?"

NIL is an incredible bonus. But **fit is the foundation.**

College NIL Readiness Checklist

My social media is clean, consistent, and aligned with my brand

- I understand the basics of NIL deals, taxes, and compliance

- I've researched the NIL rules in the NCAA and in specific states
- I have 5–7 questions ready to ask during college visits
- I've looked into the NIL collectives or athlete support programs at target schools
- I know the difference between short-term money and long-term opportunity
- I have talked with my family, coach, or mentor about choosing a school beyond NIL
- I'm building relationships—not just chasing offers
- I'm thinking like a leader, not just a recruit

Final Thoughts: Choose Growth, Not Just Glamour

The best NIL decision you can make isn't about what school offers the most money up front. It's about **which school will help you grow the most over time.**

Choose a school where:

- You can become the best version of yourself
- You're seen, supported, and developed
- Your values align with the team culture
- NIL is part of the journey—not the entire reason for being there

Because at the end of the day, your goal isn't just to win games. It's to win **in life**—and NIL is just one of many tools to help you get there.

Chapter 15: Long-Term Wealth Building Starts Now

B*ecause smart money moves at 17 can change your family tree.*

NIL might seem like a short-term win—cash for a post, a few hundred bucks from a local brand, maybe even a bigger deal if you're lucky. But here's the truth:

It's not about how much you make. It's about what you do with it.

Your NIL money can buy you sneakers, or it can buy you stock.

It can pay for a party, or it can fund your future.

It can disappear—or it can multiply.

This chapter is about how to make that second option your reality.

We're going to talk about generational wealth, investing early, and how to start building money moves now that most people don't learn until they're 30—or never at all.

What Is Generational Wealth?

Generational wealth means money, assets, or resources that are passed down from one generation to the next.

Think of it as a relay race: instead of starting from scratch, your kids and grandkids start from where you finish. You run your leg—and then pass the baton.

That could mean:

- Leaving behind savings or investments
- Passing on a business or brand you built
- Teaching your family how money works
- Paying for college or helping them start debt-free
- Owning land, property, or intellectual property (like content or patents)

Why It Matters for You:

You don't need to be a millionaire to build generational wealth. You just need to be **intentional**. You need to make smart decisions with small amounts now—so they grow into bigger opportunities later.

Your NIL money isn't just "extra" cash. It's your chance to **plant seeds** that could grow for decades.

Use Early NIL Money for College, Investing, or Business

1. Paying for College (Yes, Even If You Have a Scholarship)

NIL money can cover:

- Room and board (not always covered by athletic scholarships)
- Books, laptops, and class fees
- Travel for visits, career events, or internships
- Starting a savings fund for grad school or certifications

Even if you're on a full ride, having extra financial flexibility means **less debt and more freedom**.

> *Pro tip: Open a 529 College Savings Plan or use a high-yield savings account to store education-focused funds.*

2. Investing in the Market

Instead of just stacking cash in a checking account, you can **start investing** in:

- **Roth IRAs (we'll explain next)**
- Index funds and ETFs (like the S&P 500)
- Dividend-paying stocks

Why now matters: Time is your biggest advantage. If you start investing at 17—even $500—it could grow into tens of thousands by the time you're 40, thanks to **compound interest**.

3. Investing in Yourself (aka Entrepreneurship)

You can also use NIL income to fund:

- Your own merchandise line
- Equipment for content creation (camera, laptop, editing software)
- A camp, training service, or speaking tour
- A business idea unrelated to sports

This is how you **turn NIL into ownership.**

The Power of Roth IRAs and Compound Interest (Yes, Even at 17!)

What's a Roth IRA?

A **Roth IRA (Individual Retirement Account)** lets you invest **after-tax money**—and when you retire, your withdrawals (including profits) are **100% tax-free**.

- You can contribute **up to $7,000/year** (as of 2024) if you've earned that much income
- You can invest that money in stocks, ETFs, or mutual funds
- Your account grows over decades—**tax-free**

Why It's Perfect for Student-Athletes:

- You're probably in a low tax bracket now
- You may not have major expenses yet
- You have more **time to let your money grow** than almost anyone else

Example:

Let's say you earn $2,000 in NIL deals at age 17 and invest it into a Roth IRA:

- You never touch that money again.
- It grows at an average of **8% per year**.
- By age 65, it's worth over **$100,000**—from just that one $2,000 investment.
- Now imagine doing that **every year** from 17 to 25.

> *That's the power of compound interest:* ***your money makes money—without you working harder.***

Thinking Long-Term When Everyone Else Is Living for the Moment

Let's be real. Most people your age (and even older) are:

- Spending every dollar they get
- Chasing attention instead of assets
- Living for likes, not legacies
- Focused on flexing, not investing

You can be different.

You're Not Missing Out—You're Setting Up

While others are blowing money on trends, you're:

- **Building credit**
- **Funding a business**
- **Learning financial skills** that will serve you for life
- **Buying time and freedom** for your future family

And that doesn't mean you can't enjoy yourself. It just means you're **choosing discipline now—so you don't have to panic later.**

Wealth-Building Game Plan for High School Athletes

- Track all NIL income (know what's coming in—and where it's going)
- Set aside 20–30% for taxes (always!)
- Use a budget to save, spend, and invest with purpose
- Open a Roth IRA and contribute what you can (even $50/month)
- Learn about compound interest and start early
- Avoid debt when possible—especially credit card debt
- Think before every big purchase: "Will this help me build or just spend?"

- Reinvest part of your income in your business, content, or education
- Set a financial goal that's 10 years away—and work toward it

Final Word: Play the Long Game

You might not feel rich now.

You might not even feel like an entrepreneur or investor.

But if you've made it this far in the book, here's what you are:

- **Focused**
- **Future-minded**
- **Financially dangerous in the best way possible**

Most people never get the chance to earn income from their name as a teenager.

Even fewer know how to **use that money to create freedom.**

You do.

So don't just play to win this season.

Play to win the next decade.

And start today—because **long-term wealth building starts right now.**

Chapter 16: NIL and Community Impact

Because real influence goes beyond the screen.

You might think NIL is all about you—your brand, your deals, your content, your income. But the truth is, NIL isn't just about what you get. It's about what you give.

As a student-athlete, especially one gaining attention through NIL, you already have **influence**—even if you don't realize it yet.

Younger athletes look up to you.

Classmates respect your work ethic.

Local businesses and community members are starting to notice your name.

And the more visibility you gain, the more power you have to make **positive impact**.

This chapter will show you how to use your NIL platform not just to build wealth, but to build **character, connection, and community.**

How to Use Your Influence to Uplift Others

You don't have to be famous to make a difference.

You don't need 100,000 followers to inspire someone.

Sometimes, **showing up with intention** is all it takes.

Small Ways to Make a Big Impact:

- Shout out a younger athlete's performance on your story
- Attend a local youth league game or practice
- Visit your former middle school or elementary school
- Share words of encouragement in a group chat, DM, or post
- Use your social media to spread awareness about causes you care about

Your platform is like a microphone. The more you grow, the louder your voice becomes—so make sure you're **amplifying the right things.**

Volunteering, Mentoring, and Giving Back as Part of Your Brand

Giving back isn't just charity—it's leadership.

And in NIL, leadership builds brand equity.

Many student-athletes think their brand is just highlights and hashtags—but the most powerful brands have **heart.**

Here's how to build community service into your NIL identity:

Volunteer in Your Hometown

- Join a local food drive or community cleanup
- Support a nonprofit or youth organization that aligns with your story
- Post about it—not for clout, but to **inspire others** to get involved too

Start Mentoring Younger Athletes

- Host free mini-clinics or Q&A sessions
- Offer advice through social media posts or YouTube videos
- Become a big brother/sister figure to someone who reminds you of you

Include Giving in Your Brand Story

- Mention causes you care about in your bio or interviews
- Create "brand pillars" that include service, mentorship, or impact
- Show how you're not just taking opportunities—you're creating them for others

> *Real talk:* ***Helping others doesn't take away from your NIL—it adds to it.*** *Brands want to work with athletes who have purpose. Communities support athletes who give back. Coaches notice players who care about more than just themselves.*

NIL Opportunities Tied to Charity Work and Local Causes

Not all NIL deals are about selling products—some are about **promoting purpose**.

Examples of Cause-Driven NIL:

- A local gym partners with you to promote a charity 5K run
- A smoothie shop offers to donate a portion of sales to a cause you choose during your sponsored week
- A brand pays you to raise awareness for youth mental health, childhood cancer, or literacy
- You donate 10% of your merch profits to a nonprofit you believe in—and the brand shares your impact story

Tip: Bring Your Own Ideas

You don't have to wait for someone to offer a deal. You can **pitch your own cause-driven campaigns.**

Try this format when reaching out to a brand:

> *"I'm a local student-athlete with a growing platform and a passion for [cause]. I'd love to explore a partnership where we collaborate to support [charity/event]—and show how NIL can do more than just sell products. Would you be open to discussing a campaign that creates impact and visibility for both of us?"*

That message says:

- I have a mission
- I understand marketing
- I want to create a win-win

That's what separates a regular NIL athlete from a visionary.

Building Character and Credibility Through Community Engagement

What you build in your community says more about you than what you post online.

Character isn't just what you show in a game—it's how you show up **when there's nothing to gain.**

NIL has given you a spotlight. But **your service is what gives it meaning.**

The Benefits of Community Impact:

- **Credibility:** People believe in who you are—not just what you do
- **Trust:** Brands, schools, and mentors respect your leadership
- **Legacy:** You become more than a good player—you become a role model
- **Fulfillment:** You feel more connected, grounded, and purposeful

Whether you're mentoring one kid, helping a neighborhood initiative, or raising awareness for a cause—**you are building a name that means something.**

Community Impact Game Plan for Student-Athletes

Choose 1 cause you care about (faith, health, education, equity, etc.)

- Follow local nonprofits, youth centers, or community groups on social media
- Reach out to volunteer or attend their events
- Share one story or moment from your experience on your own platform
- Include community service in your bio, media kit, or NIL resume
- Talk to a coach or mentor about starting a school-wide service campaign
- Reinvest part of your NIL income in your cause (even $20 makes a difference)
- Ask a local brand to partner with you on a cause-based campaign
- Reflect: "How do I want to be remembered when the game is over?"

Final Word: Use the Platform—Don't Just Perform on It

The truth is, people may not remember every touchdown, dunk, or goal you ever scored.

But they'll remember:

- The time you visited their kid's classroom
- The way you gave back to your school
- The moment you stood for something beyond yourself

Your NIL platform can give you influence—but **your choices determine what you do with it.**

So don't just play for fame.

Don't just post for followers.

Lead with impact. Serve with purpose. Build with heart.

Because what you give will always echo louder than what you get.

Chapter 17: NIL and Mental Health – Protecting Your Mind While Building Your Brand

The NIL world can feel like a dream come true—money, recognition, influence. But with all that opportunity comes pressure. Pressure to perform. Pressure to look a certain way. Pressure to say the right thing. Pressure to always be "on."

Let's be real: getting paid and gaining followers doesn't mean life gets easier—it just means the problems change.

And if you're not careful, chasing the bag can leave you drained, anxious, and unsure of who you really are.

This chapter is about protecting your mind while you build your NIL brand. Because mental wealth matters just as much as financial wealth.

You're More Than a Brand

The moment you start monetizing your name, image, and likeness, you may feel like *you* become the product. Likes, shares, impressions, and endorsements become part of your identity. You start asking:

- "Am I doing enough?"
- "Why didn't that post get more engagement?"
- "What if I say the wrong thing?"

But here's the truth: **you are more than your stats, your social media, or your sponsorships**. You're a person first—an athlete second—and a brand last.

Keep that order in check.

The Silent Stress of NIL

NIL success brings silent stressors that aren't always talked about:

- **Constant comparison:** Watching teammates or rivals land bigger deals can feel discouraging.
- **Decision fatigue:** Juggling school, sports, NIL opportunities, and personal life is exhausting.
- **Fear of missing out (FOMO):** You might feel pressure to say yes to every opportunity—even if you're not ready.
- **Public scrutiny:** Every post, story, and move you make is under the microscope.

All of these can quietly chip away at your confidence, your focus, and your peace of mind.

Signs Your Mental Health Needs Attention

It's important to know when to hit pause. Pay attention if you start noticing:

- Trouble sleeping or eating
- Constant feelings of being overwhelmed or anxious
- Loss of motivation in your sport or schoolwork
- Isolating from friends or teammates
- Feelings of sadness or hopelessness

These aren't just "bad days"—they could be signs you need support. There is no shame in that. Real strength is recognizing when something isn't right and doing something about it.

How to Set Boundaries in the NIL World

Boundaries are your best defense in the NIL space. Here are a few to consider:

- **Time boundaries:** Block off hours where you're off your phone, off email, and focused on recovery, class, or family.
- **Brand boundaries:** Know what you're willing to promote and what doesn't align with your values.
- **People boundaries:** Not everyone gets access to you—be careful who you let into your circle.

Boundaries = protection. And protection keeps you sane.

Build Your Mental Health Team, Too

Just like you need a lawyer for your contracts and a CPA for your taxes, you need **support for your mental health**:

- **Sports psychologist or therapist**
- **Academic advisors and mentors**
- **Trusted family and friends**
- **Coaches who respect the full person, not just the player**

Normalize check-ins, therapy, and talking about what you're going through.

The Role of Social Media in Mental Health

Social media is a powerful NIL tool—but it can also be mentally toxic if you let it run you.

Here's how to keep your relationship with social media healthy:

- Don't tie your worth to your engagement numbers
- Unfollow accounts that make you feel less-than
- Limit your screen time
- Take breaks without feeling guilty
- Avoid arguing or reading hateful comments

You control the app—don't let it control you.

Daily Habits That Protect Your Peace

Just like you train your body, train your mind. Build habits that protect your peace:

- **Sleep:** Non-negotiable. Aim for 7–9 hours.
- **Journaling:** Reflect on wins, goals, and what's weighing you down.
- **Exercise for joy, not just performance.**
- **Gratitude practice:** Write down 3 things you're thankful for every day.
- **Quiet time:** Prayer, meditation, or just sitting still.

These aren't "extras"—they're part of your self-care game plan.

It's Okay to Say No

You don't have to accept every NIL deal. You don't have to post every day. You don't have to be perfect.

You have permission to say no to things that don't feel right or add unnecessary stress.

Protect your peace, your privacy, and your energy.

When NIL Isn't Fun Anymore

If NIL ever starts to feel like a burden instead of a blessing—step back. Talk to someone. Recenter.

This is supposed to be a tool for opportunity, not something that steals your joy.

There will be other deals. There will be other moments. But you only get one you.

Final Thoughts: Mental Wealth = Real Wealth

You can't perform at your best or make smart money moves if your mind isn't right.

Protect your mental health the same way you protect your bag.

Because in the end, **mental wealth is part of your legacy too.**

Chapter 18: Contracts, Agents, and the Fine Print

Let's talk contracts—the papers you sign that can either secure your future or mess it up fast.

In the NIL world, **contracts are everywhere**: sponsorships, content deals, appearances, licensing agreements, brand ambassadorships, and more. You might even be approached by agents or companies promising to "blow up your brand."

Sounds exciting, right? But here's the truth: **if you don't understand what you're signing, you might be giving away more than you realize**—your time, your money, your name, your image, even your future earnings.

This chapter will show you how to protect yourself by learning how to spot red flags, understand your rights, and know when to ask for help.

Why You Need to Read Every Word

Don't just scroll to the signature line. Contracts are legally binding documents. Once you sign, you're locked in—whether you understood it or not.

Ask yourself:

- What exactly am I agreeing to?
- For how long?

- What do they get? What do I get?
- What happens if I don't deliver—or if they don't?

If you can't answer those questions, you're not ready to sign.

Key Contract Terms You Must Know

Here are some common terms you'll see in NIL contracts—learn them like you learn your playbook:

- **Term (or Duration):** How long the contract lasts.
- **Exclusivity:** Are you allowed to work with other brands?
- **Compensation:** How much you'll be paid—and how.
- **Deliverables:** What are you required to do? (Posts? Appearances? Events?)
- **Usage Rights:** Can the brand use your name/image forever—even after the deal ends?
- **Termination Clause:** How can either side end the contract early?
- **Morality Clause:** Can you get dropped for saying or doing something the brand doesn't like?

These are just the basics. Contracts can be long and confusing on purpose—that's why you've got to slow down and ask questions.

Red Flags in NIL Contracts

Not all contracts are fair. Here are some warning signs that something might be off:

- Vague language like "at the company's discretion"
- No clear payment structure or timeline
- No termination clause or way for *you* to exit the deal
- Promises that sound too good to be true

- Being rushed or pressured to sign quickly
- No room for negotiation ("take it or leave it")
- Lack of detail about what's expected from both sides

If you feel something's off—it probably is.

What About Agents, Reps, and Collectives?

You might get approached by:

- **Agents** (who negotiate deals for you)
- **Marketing Reps** (who "help build your brand")
- **NIL Collectives** (groups that pool funds to support athletes at a school)

Sounds great, but be careful. Some people want to help you—others want to help themselves.

Before signing with anyone:

- **Ask if they're licensed** (agents must be registered in some states)
- **Ask who else they've worked with**
- **Ask about their commission** (most take 10–20%—but it should be spelled out)
- **Ask how and when you can leave the relationship**
- **Ask if your school has approved or vetted them**

Just because someone has followers doesn't mean they're trustworthy.

What You Own (and What You Might Give Away)

When you sign an NIL contract, you're often giving a brand permission to use your:

- Name

- Image
- Likeness
- Voice
- Social handles
- Photos and videos
- Athletic performance

Be clear on what they can use—and for how long. Some contracts try to claim *lifetime* rights, even after you leave college. Don't give away your future just to get free gear or a small check now.

When to Get a Lawyer or Advisor Involved

Here's a simple rule: **If the contract is longer than a page, has big money involved, or makes you nervous—get help.**

You can talk to:

- A family attorney
- A school-provided legal resource or compliance officer
- A licensed sports agent
- A NIL-focused advisor

It's worth paying $100 to have someone read your contract *before* you sign—**especially if it could cost you thousands down the road.**

Your Rights as a Student-Athlete

Even in the NIL world, you still have rights:

- You don't have to work with anyone you don't trust
- You don't have to sign exclusivity unless it's clear and fair
- You can walk away from shady deals
- You can (and should) ask questions about every part of a contract

- You always have the right to *protect your name*

Just because you're young doesn't mean you're powerless.

What Happens If You Break the Contract?

Sometimes, stuff happens:

- You miss a post
- You get injured
- You transfer schools
- You stop liking the brand

What happens next depends on your **termination clause**. You might owe money back. You might get dropped. You might get sued (worst case).

This is why it's so important to read the *exit terms* of the contract before you sign.

Final Tips Before You Sign Anything

1. **Take your time.** Don't let anyone rush you.
2. **Google the company.** Make sure they're legit.
3. **Keep a copy of everything.** Email it to yourself and a trusted adult.
4. **Ask for clarification.** If something's unclear, ask for it in writing.
5. **Remember your value.** Just because you're in high school or college doesn't mean your brand is cheap.

Final Thoughts: Protect the Brand Called "YOU"

NIL deals are business—and business means contracts. If you treat this seriously now, you'll save yourself stress, regret, and lost money later.

Every contract is an agreement with your future. Don't sign something that puts that future at risk.

Because at the end of the day—your name is your brand, and your brand is your legacy.

Chapter 19: Managing Peer Pressure and Lifestyle Inflation

So you got your first NIL deal. You've got some money coming in. Maybe a brand sent you free gear. Maybe people on campus are starting to recognize you more. You're *on the rise.*

But here comes the pressure...

- "Bro, you should cop those new kicks."
- "Let's go out this weekend—you got it."
- "You really flying coach now?"
- "You're NIL now... you can pay for it."

Here's the problem: **once the money starts flowing, people expect you to start flexing.** Welcome to the world of **peer pressure and lifestyle inflation**—two silent money killers.

If you don't get a handle on this early, your NIL opportunity will disappear as fast as it came.

What Is Lifestyle Inflation?

Lifestyle inflation is when your spending grows just because your income does. You start upgrading everything:

- Your wardrobe

- Your phone
- Your meals
- Your travel
- Your car

It's the "I make more, so I *deserve* more" mentality. And while that feels good short-term, it **kills your long-term goals**—especially when NIL money isn't guaranteed year to year.

Peer Pressure: The Silent Wallet Drainer

Most athletes don't go broke because they don't make money—they go broke trying to keep up.

You'll feel pressure from:

- **Friends:** "Come on, just spot me."
- **Social media:** "They're doing it, why not me?"
- **Family:** "Can you help with [fill in the blank]?"
- **Your own expectations:** "I earned this. I should enjoy it."

But here's the truth: **real wealth is quiet**. It's peace of mind, not flashy outfits. It's knowing your bills are paid, not impressing people who don't contribute to your future.

Signs You're Caught in the Trap

- You're always "broke" even though you just got paid
- You buy things to feel better when you're stressed
- You're afraid to post a "normal" moment because it doesn't look rich enough
- You've loaned money to friends or family that hasn't come back
- You feel anxious when you can't spend like others around you

If any of those hit home, pause. Breathe. You're not alone—and you can take back control.

Strategies to Stay Grounded

Let's build your defense plan.

1. Set Personal Financial Goals

Before the pressure hits, know what *you* want:

- Save $5,000 before graduation
- Start a Roth IRA
- Pay off your car
- Launch your own brand
- Help your family—but on *your terms*

When you have a plan, it's easier to say no to distractions.

2. Create a "Yes, No, Maybe" List

- **YES:** Things worth spending on (e.g., quality equipment, business investments, experiences that matter).
- **NO:** Flashy stuff to impress others, parties you don't enjoy, unnecessary subscriptions.
- **MAYBE:** Big purchases that require a waiting period (give it 7 days—if you still want it, then decide).

3. Practice Saying "Not Right Now"

You don't have to say *never*—you just have to say *not today*.

- "I'm focused on something bigger right now."
- "That's not in my budget this month."
- "I'm stacking for something important."

If they're really your people, they'll respect it. If not, they were using you anyway.

4. Create a Separate Spending Account

Put your NIL money in an account that's harder to access. Set up automatic transfers to savings or investments. What you don't see, you won't spend.

Social Media: The Highlight Reel Trap

Don't let IG trick you into thinking everyone else is living better than you.

- That car might be leased
- That trip might be sponsored
- That "luxury lifestyle" might be debt

Post what's real. Live what's realer.

You don't need to prove anything to anyone but your future self.

Handling Friends Who Always Ask for Money

Money changes relationships. Some friends may:

- Assume you'll always pay
- Guilt you for having more
- Ask for "small" loans that never come back

Here's a tip: **Have a "No Loan Policy."** If you give money, think of it as a gift you don't expect back. Better yet, **offer opportunities, not handouts**:

- "I can help you with a resume."
- "Here's where I learned about money."
- "Let's build something together."

You can support people without going broke.

Build a Money Mindset Bigger Than the Moment

Here's the truth: **being rich isn't about what you wear—it's about what you *own*.**

That means:

- Owning your time
- Owning your decisions
- Owning your financial future

Don't trade long-term peace for short-term pressure.

Reflection Questions

1. Who do I feel pressure to impress?
2. What am I spending money on that doesn't align with my goals?
3. How can I set better boundaries with friends, family, and social media?
4. What financial habits can I build to stay focused?

Final Thoughts: Stay True to You

NIL gives you options. But it also comes with responsibility. The more grounded you stay, the more powerful your decisions become.

Don't flex for the timeline. Stack for the future.

Because real success? **It shows up when the lights are off, the cameras are gone, and your bank account still has your back.**

Chapter 20: Culture: The Lens That Shapes How You See Money

Financial literacy doesn't begin with a budget or a bank account. It begins with your story. It begins with how you were raised, what you were exposed to, and the experiences — good or bad — that shaped your relationship with money.

Let's keep it real: depending on your race, gender, religion, upbringing, and environment, you're going to see money through a different lens than the person next to you. And that's okay. In fact, it's *essential* to understand this if you're going to build wealth that lasts.

Your Lens Is Unique

If you were raised by a single mom holding down multiple jobs just to put food on the table, where the only conversations about money were about not having enough of it, then *of course* your relationship with money is different. You may feel pressure to earn as much as possible, as fast as possible. You might struggle with guilt when spending or saving because scarcity was the norm.

If you grew up in a neighborhood where drug dealers drove the nicest cars and wore the nicest clothes — and sports was your only way out — then yeah, money might represent freedom, status, or even survival. That's your lens. Your hustle was born from survival. But now, it's time to pivot from *survival mode* to *wealth mode*.

If you found out, years later, that your uncle or someone close to you used your Social Security number and racked up thousands in debt before you were even 18 — then trust issues around money are valid. That betrayal can shape how much you trust banks, credit systems, and even professionals.

No matter what your background is — Black, white, brown, green — *it all comes down to exposure.* Exposure to knowledge. Exposure to what's possible. Exposure to the tools that weren't handed to you growing up.

You Can't Change Where You Come From — But You Can Change Where You're Going

The way forward starts with educating yourself, and this book is part of that journey. Don't let anyone — not your coach, your agent, your accountant, or even your teammate — tell you that financial literacy isn't for you. *You* are your first line of defense.

People will tell you "that's your financial advisor's job" or "your agent will take care of that." Nah. Make them teach you.

- If you have a financial advisor — ask them to break it down.
- If you're working with a CPA — understand your taxes.
- If you have an agent or a manager — demand transparency in your deals.

Every professional on your team works *for* you. But if you don't understand the playbook, how will you know if they're running the right plays?

Learn the Game — So You Don't Get Played

Every year, we see headlines about athletes — even pros — who get taken advantage of. Millions lost. Careers cut short. Financial ruin. The saddest part? In most cases, it wasn't because they didn't *make* enough money. It's because they didn't *understand* what was being done with it.

This is why culture matters. If you were taught to keep quiet, to trust the system, or to avoid talking about money altogether — *break that cycle*. Ask questions. Get uncomfortable. Demand answers.

Read this book. Read *other* books. Listen to podcasts. Watch YouTube videos. Take courses. You don't have to be a finance major to understand your own money. You just have to *care enough to learn.*

This Is Bigger Than You

Let's be real — you might be the first in your family to have a shot at real money. You might be the first to sign an NIL deal, to start a business, or to even think about generational wealth. That's not pressure — that's *power.*

Learn the game so you can teach it to your younger siblings, cousins, teammates, or even your future kids. Be the one who changes the narrative in your family and your community.

Final Word

Your culture shaped how you first viewed money. But your mindset will determine what you *do* with it. Don't let your past limit your future. Whether you come from privilege or pain, you have the right to financial literacy. You have the power to understand. And you have the responsibility to take control.

Because when you understand money, you don't just win on the field — you win in life.

Money = Options

Most people live paycheck to paycheck. Not because they're lazy or reckless—but because they never learned how to plan, save, and invest early. They get stuck working jobs they hate, signing bad contracts, or making decisions out of desperation instead of strategy.

When you save and invest now, you build a cushion—and that cushion gives you room to breathe. You won't have to take every deal just for the money. You can:

- Start your own business
- Go back to school
- Travel
- Help your family
- Support causes you care about
- Invest in real estate or other people's ideas

Saving money gives you time.

Investing money gives you leverage.

Together, they give you options.

Small Moves = Big Results

You don't need millions to start. You just need consistency.

Let's say you invest just $150/month starting at age 20. That's $1,800 a year—less than what many student-athletes make from a single NIL post. If you do that for 30 years and earn an average of 8% per year, you'll have around $220,000 by age 50.

If you increase that to $300/month? Now you're looking at over $440,000.

That's not even pro athlete money—it's future-proof money.

Your Future Self Will Thank You

When you're 20, the decisions you make might feel small. But they're not. You're laying the foundation. And just like training, reps now pay off later.

Imagine being 30 and having enough invested to take a year off to travel.

Imagine being 40 and owning two rental properties that generate passive income.

Imagine being 50 and choosing to work—or not—because you planned for it.

None of that happens by accident. It starts now, with the money you earn through NIL or summer jobs, and what you decide to do with it.

Final Word: The Sooner You Start, the More Choices You'll Have

Money isn't everything—but it makes everything easier when used wisely.

If you save and invest with discipline now, you'll have choices that most people only dream of.

Give your future self the gift of options.

Be the athlete today who builds the freedom to live life on your terms tomorrow.

Use NIL to Launch Your Next Career, Not Just a Lifestyle

Right now, you've got something rare: a platform, an audience, and income through NIL. You're building a brand, getting paid for your influence, and maybe even getting free gear, endorsements, and opportunities that most people your age never experience.

But here's the real question:

Are you using your NIL to build a lifestyle—or to launch a career?

Buying new clothes, traveling, upgrading your car—those things feel good in the moment. They give you that sense of success. But if the money stops tomorrow, does the progress stop too?

Lifestyle fades. Careers last.

NIL Isn't Just a Payday—It's a Platform

NIL deals aren't just checks—they're introductions. They're chances to connect with brands, CEOs, entrepreneurs, creators, alumni, and future business partners. If you're intentional, your NIL journey can double as a launchpad for whatever comes next.

Here's how:

- Turn partnerships into relationships
- Don't just take the check and disappear. Follow up. Thank the brand. Ask how else you can collaborate. Show you're about business, not just hype.
- Build a portfolio
- Every NIL campaign you do is a case study. Screenshot it. Save the stats. Create a digital résumé showing what you've done and the value you brought. That can lead to marketing jobs, consulting work, and future brand deals.
- Explore industries that interest you
- Like fitness? Partner with gyms and wellness companies.
- Into fashion? Work with apparel brands and learn the design or production side.
- Love content? Build your media brand and learn how editing, SEO, and monetization really work.

Use NIL to test-drive careers—not just to cash in.

Fund Your Future

Your NIL earnings can also help you:

- Start a business
- Pay for certifications or grad school
- Invest in real estate or a retirement account
- Hire a mentor or coach to level up your knowledge
- Take an unpaid internship you otherwise couldn't afford

Most people grind for years to save enough money to take these kinds of risks. You're in a position to do it now—if you're smart.

Your Career Starts Now

You don't have to wait until the game ends to figure out what's next. In fact, you shouldn't. The habits, relationships, and moves you make now will either open doors—or keep you scrambling when the lights go out.

You have a chance to walk out of college not just with a degree, but with a brand, a business, and a blueprint for what's next. That's what winning off the field really looks like.

Final Word: Cashing Out Is Cool—Cashing In on Your Future Is Smarter

You worked too hard to let NIL be just a moment.

Use it as a movement.

Build something that outlasts the trends.

Use NIL not just to live—use it to launch.

Conclusion: Winning Off the Field

You came into this book because you care about your future. You're not just here for the short-term wins—you're here to play the long game. And now, you've got the tools, the mindset, and the knowledge to do exactly that.

NIL has changed the landscape. It's opened doors that generations before you didn't have access to. You have opportunities to earn, to build, to brand, and to lead in ways most college students can only imagine. But with those opportunities come choices—and the way you handle those choices now will shape the rest of your life.

You've learned how to manage your money, track your income, avoid taxes hitting like a blindside blitz, and invest early so your future self has options. You've learned how to treat yourself like a business—not just an athlete—and how to build a support network, protect your brand, and plan for life after sports.

But more than that, you've learned that real success isn't about the moment—it's about what comes after it.

The wins that matter most won't be listed in box scores. They'll show up in the freedom you create for yourself.

- The freedom to walk away from bad deals
- The freedom to take a chance on your dream
- The freedom to support your family, your community, and yourself—without stress

That's what financial literacy is all about. It's not about being rich just to say you are.

It's about being in control—of your money, your time, your decisions, and your life.

Because when the last game ends, when the jersey comes off, when the followers slow down, and the cameras point elsewhere—you'll still be here. And how you prepared while the spotlight was on will determine what happens next.

You've already proven that you're dedicated. You've shown up to early morning lifts, pushed through tough practices, bounced back from setbacks, and stayed hungry when things got hard.

Now it's time to apply that same energy to your financial life.

To your business.

To your future.

Final Word: Your Legacy Is Bigger Than Your Stats

Your legacy won't just be what you did on the field. It'll be what you built after the game.

Will you be the athlete who blew the bag—or the one who flipped it into something that lasts?

Will you spend your NIL moment chasing clout—or building your career?

That choice is yours.

But remember this:

Winning off the field takes vision, discipline, and consistency—just like winning on it.

And if you're reading this, you already have what it takes.

So go be great.

Not just on game day—but every day.

This is your life. This is your brand. This is your legacy.

Now go win it. Off the field. For good.

Success Isn't a Highlight Reel—It's What Happens Off-Camera

We live in a world where it's easy to confuse success with attention.

You post a clip. It gets likes. You sign an NIL deal. You get followers. You score big in a game. You go viral. It *looks* like you're winning—and in many ways, you are.

But real success? The kind that lasts?

It happens off-camera.

It's what you do when no one's watching.

It's in the choices you make after the lights go out.

It's in the discipline of budgeting when the money hits your account.

It's in saying "no" to the shiny, short-term purchase so you can say "yes" to long-term freedom.

It's in the extra hour you spend learning how investing works, while others scroll past it.

Highlights are loud. They flash across screens and get reposted. But the real wins—the ones that build generational wealth, stability, peace of mind, and opportunity—those are quiet. Steady. Behind the scenes.

You're More Than the Clips

What the world sees:

- The brand deals
- The gear
- The followers
- The stats
- The smiles

What they don't see:

- You researching what a Roth IRA is
- You setting up a meeting with a financial advisor
- You saying no to that third trip this month because you're focused on saving
- You staying in to finish a pitch deck, write a business plan, or build your personal brand

That's the work that doesn't get likes—but it gets results.

Long-Term Success Is Built in the Shadows

Every legendary athlete has moments the fans never see. The late-night lifts. The rehab sessions. The quiet self-doubt. The film study after everyone else has gone home.

Your financial success is no different.

Every time you track your expenses, contribute to your investment account, or ask a mentor for guidance, you're stacking invisible wins. You're laying a foundation that doesn't show up on the timeline—but will show up when it matters most.

Final Thought: Chase Legacy, Not Just Hype

Don't get caught living for the highlight reel. Because once the game is over and the noise fades, what you're left with is what you built behind the scenes.

Money comes and goes. Trends fade. But discipline? Knowledge? Ownership?

Those things last.

So let others chase the flash.

You? Chase the foundation. The freedom. The future.

Because success isn't just the crowd cheering—it's the quiet moment when you look at your bank account, your business, your peace of mind, and you smile...

knowing you played the real game right.

Off-camera. Off the field.

And still winning.

Don't Take Advice from Just Anyone—Especially Not Your Uncle Who Teaches 7th Grade Math (No Offense)

Let's be real. Once you start making money, everyone suddenly becomes a financial expert.

Your teammate tells you to invest in crypto.

Your friend swears by some sketchy NFT.

Your uncle—who teaches 7th grade math and drives a 20-year-old minivan—starts talking to you about "flipping houses" and "how back in his day..."

Listen, no offense to your uncle. He's probably a great guy, a solid teacher, and someone who means well. But when it comes to managing NIL money, building wealth, or launching your business brand?

You need more than good intentions. You need expertise.

The Cost of Bad Advice

The wrong advice doesn't just waste your time—it can cost you thousands of dollars. It can delay your goals, ruin your credit, or leave you with a tax mess that takes years to fix.

Not everyone who cares about you knows what they're talking about when it comes to:

- Taxes and deductions
- Investment strategy
- LLC formation
- NIL contract terms
- Insurance coverage
- Budgeting for fluctuating income

Just because someone "heard it on YouTube" or "did it one time in the '90s" doesn't mean it applies to your situation in 2025.

Get Your Financial Advice from Real Professionals

You wouldn't let someone who's never played a down coach your team, right?

Then why take financial advice from someone who's never managed six-figure income, reviewed a contract, or filed a self-employment tax return?

When it comes to your money, your team matters.

Work with professionals who understand:

- NIL rules and regulations

- Student-athlete eligibility concerns
- Taxes for self-employed individuals
- How to help you plan for both now and the future

This includes:

- Certified Financial Planners (CFPs)
- CPAs with NIL or athlete experience
- NIL agents who've worked with other student-athletes
- Attorneys who specialize in contract and intellectual property law

You Can Still Love Your Uncle—Just Don't Bank on His Advice

Let the uncle teach math class. Let your teammate be hype on Instagram. Let your roommate invest in meme coins if they want.

But you? You're building something real.

Ask questions. Be curious. But always check the credentials.

Because when it comes to money, legacy, and long-term wealth, guessing isn't good enough.

Final Word: Respect Everyone. Listen to a Few. Choose the Right Ones.

Take advice from people who are where you want to be—not just people who talk loud.

This is your money, your brand, your future.

Get your game plan from pros, not just your people.

Surround Yourself with Professionals Who Know the Game

Every great athlete has a team behind the scenes: coaches, trainers, film guys, nutritionists, therapists, mentors—the people who don't make the highlight reel but make everything else possible.

Your financial life should be the same way.

You need a team.

Not just hype people, but professionals—advisors, accountants, attorneys, and mentors who understand your goals and know how to guide you through the game of money.

Because here's the truth:

Winning off the field takes a game plan—and the right people to help you execute it.

Not Everyone Knows the Athlete Life—But Some Do

You don't need a suit who's never touched a field telling you how to live.

You need someone who's been there. Someone who understands what it's like to juggle school, sports, pressure, and now, business.

Someone who's walked in your cleats—and still knows how to build wealth, structure deals, and protect your future.

That's where people like Pat Brown, MBA, come in.

Pat isn't just a money guy. He's a former Division I football player who knows what it's like to be in your shoes—and more importantly, what it takes to be successful once those shoes come off.

After competing at the highest levels and briefly playing professionally, Pat shifted his energy toward a different kind of game: helping student-athletes win with their money.

He's built multiple financial education platforms, speaks nationally to athletes, and is a trusted advocate for young people navigating the new NIL era. From budgeting and taxes to investing and entrepreneurship, Pat helps athletes like you move with strategy—not stress.

Who You Surround Yourself With = Who You Become

If you only take advice from people who are winging it, you'll end up winging it too.

But when you put smart, experienced people in your circle—people who understand NIL, contracts, money, and mindset—you position yourself to make moves, not mistakes.

The right people will help you:

- Avoid tax traps
- Invest wisely
- Protect your brand
- Start your business the right way
- Build wealth that lasts long after the cheers fade

This isn't about being flashy. It's about being future-ready.

Final Word: Find People Who Want You to Win Off the Field

Your success doesn't stop with the game—it starts when you build a life beyond it.

So surround yourself with pros who know the playbook. People who see you as more than a follower count or a stat sheet. Because champions aren't just made in the weight room.

They're built with wisdom, guidance, and the right team around them.

Keep Learning, Keep Growing, and Play to Win for Life

By now, you've realized something important: this game is bigger than sports.

Yes, you've trained your body, sharpened your skills, and competed at the highest levels. But the next stage of your journey? That's where your legacy is built.

Winning in life—*real life*—requires a new kind of playbook.

You've got to learn how money works.

You've got to protect what you're building.

You've got to prepare for the long game—not just the next paycheck, semester, or season.

But here's the best part: you already have everything inside you to do it.

You've shown up early. You've grinded. You've stayed disciplined when no one was watching. You've bounced back after losses. You've held yourself accountable.

Now, it's time to apply that same energy to your finances, your business moves, your relationships, and your mindset.

This Isn't a One-Time Play—It's a Lifelong Season

Financial literacy isn't something you learn once and forget.

It's something you practice. Just like your sport.

You're not going to master everything overnight. And that's okay. What matters is that you *keep learning.*

Keep asking questions.

Keep showing up.

Keep surrounding yourself with mentors, professionals, and people who want to see you win off the field.

No one is expecting you to be perfect. They're expecting you to be intentional.

Growth Is the Real Goal

Money will come and go. Followers rise and fall. Careers start and end.

But growth? That's forever.

The student-athlete who reads this book and takes action—starts saving, opens an investment account, asks for help, plans for life after the game—that person becomes the professional, the entrepreneur, the parent, the leader, the community builder.

That person becomes someone with options, ownership, and peace of mind.

That person becomes you.

Final Word: Play to Win for Life

You've learned what it takes to win on the field. You've pushed yourself. You've earned the right to be here.

Now it's time to take that same mindset and apply it to every area of your life.

NIL is just the beginning.

Money is just a tool.

Your sport is just one chapter.

But your life?

That's the big game.

So keep learning.

Keep growing.

Keep showing up.

And most of all—

Play to win. Not just today. Not just for likes.

Play to win for life.

You've got this. Let's go.

Chapter 21: Charitable Giving and Community Engagement

Let's flip the script for a second.

Everyone talks about how *you* can win with NIL—how you can make money, build your brand, and create opportunities. But what if part of your success included **lifting other people up, too?**

That's what this chapter is about: **giving back in a way that makes sense, feels right, and fits your mission.** Not out of pressure. Not for likes. But because when you give with intention, *everybody wins*—including you.

Why Giving Back Is a Power Move

Charitable giving and community engagement aren't just "feel good" things. They're smart brand moves. Here's why:

- **It builds trust.** People respect athletes who stand for more than just money and self-promotion.
- **It opens doors.** Brands, schools, and organizations love to align with purpose-driven athletes.
- **It creates lasting impact.** Money comes and goes, but the difference you make in someone's life can last forever.

If you use NIL to only serve yourself, you'll run out of fuel. But if you use it to also serve others, you'll *create a legacy*.

Ways to Give Without Going Broke

You don't have to be rich to make a difference. Start where you are. Here are some ways you can give back without draining your bank account:

1. Time

- Volunteer at a youth camp or after-school program
- Mentor a younger athlete who looks up to you
- Show up to local events or speak at your former middle/high school

2. Voice

- Use your platform to raise awareness about causes you care about
- Share a GoFundMe, nonprofit, or scholarship program
- Collaborate with local organizations that align with your story

3. Energy & Skills

- Offer free training sessions or clinics
- Help with fundraisers or event planning
- Run a sports gear drive or holiday donation effort

4. Money (When You're Ready)

- Donate a portion of NIL earnings to a charity
- Sponsor a kid's team, league, or school project
- Start a scholarship fund in your name (this can come later with help from a financial advisor or foundation)

Giving is about **intention, not size**. A $20 donation done with love can mean more than a $20,000 one done for clout.

Build a Brand That's Bigger Than You

The best brands in sports today—think LeBron, Serena, Steph—aren't just known for performance. They're known for **purpose**.

You don't have to wait until you're a pro to start living that way. Start now:

- Choose causes that matter to you personally
- Share stories, not just stats
- Align with brands that reflect your values
- Make giving part of your identity, not just a once-a-year moment

Your brand becomes more **authentic, relatable, and respected** when it includes purpose.

Real Athletes Doing Real Good

Here are a few young athletes who've already made impact with their NIL platforms:

- **Hercy Miller** (Tennessee State): Donated NIL earnings to support HBCUs and underserved communities.
- **Haley and Hanna Cavinder** (Miami): Partnered with charities in tandem with brand deals to give back locally.
- **Jaden Rashada**: Helped fund youth football camps and community programs with NIL proceeds.

They didn't wait. They started where they were. So can you.

How to Choose the Right Cause

You don't have to support everything. Pick a cause that hits home:

- Mental health
- Cancer awareness
- Youth sports access
- Hunger and food insecurity
- Single-parent families
- Education and literacy

Then ask:

- "What does this have to do with my story?"
- "Would I support this even if no one knew?"
- "Can I create consistent impact—not just one-time hype?"

Start small. Stay focused. Be consistent.

Turn NIL Into a Movement, Not Just a Moment

Here's a quick idea flow:

1. **Pick a cause**
2. **Pick a platform** (event, fundraiser, social media campaign)
3. **Partner with a nonprofit** (they already have the systems and legal structures in place)
4. **Promote it with your NIL voice**
5. **Track the impact—and share the story**

You'll be amazed at the doors that open when people see your heart in action.

The Tax-Smart Way to Give

Yep—there's a financial benefit too. In many cases, donations to registered nonprofits (501(c)(3) organizations) can be **tax deductible**.

That means:

- You help others
- You build your brand
- You potentially lower your tax bill

Just make sure:

- You keep **receipts and documentation**
- You work with a **tax advisor** who understands NIL and charitable giving

Smart generosity is a win-win.

Final Thoughts: Your Legacy Starts Now

You don't have to wait until you "make it" to start making a difference.

The most powerful NIL brand is the one that **gives back while it grows**.

Because when people talk about you 10, 20, 30 years from now... they might not remember your stats.

But they'll remember your impact.

Give boldly. Give smart. Give with heart.

Chapter 22: Mistakes That Cost Athletes Millions

There's a long list of athletes who made millions... and lost it all.

We're not talking about rare exceptions either—**it happens more often than you think.** The reasons? Bad contracts. Reckless spending. Trusting the wrong people. Not paying taxes. Social media blowups. Poor planning. You name it.

But this chapter isn't here to shame anyone. It's here to help *you* avoid becoming another headline.

Because whether you make $5,000 from NIL or $5 million as a pro, **the money can vanish fast if you don't respect it**.

Let's Start with the Numbers

- According to Sports Illustrated, **78% of former NFL players** are bankrupt or under financial stress within 2 years of retirement.
- **60% of NBA players** face similar challenges within 5 years of leaving the league.
- Even Olympic athletes and top college players have gone broke before ever turning pro.

NIL may be new, but the lessons are old: **money doesn't fix your problems—it just makes your decisions more expensive.**

Mistake #1: Signing a Bad Contract

Case Study: Ricky Williams (NFL)

He signed a rookie deal with huge performance bonuses and very little guaranteed money. The structure of the contract cost him tens of millions over time.

Lesson: *Don't sign a contract you don't understand. Ever.* NIL deals can have:

- Lifetime usage rights
- Hidden exclusivity clauses
- No clear payment terms Always ask for clarification, and when in doubt—*get help* before you sign.

Mistake #2: Spending Like the Money Will Never Run Out

Case Study: Antoine Walker (NBA)

Made over $108 million in his NBA career—and filed for bankruptcy. Why? Lavish lifestyle, bad investments, and helping too many friends and family members.

Lesson: NIL money might feel like a "come up," but it can dry up fast. Lifestyle creep is real. You don't need to flex just because you can.

Mistake #3: Trusting the Wrong People

Case Study: Tim Duncan (NBA)

One of the smartest, calmest players in NBA history—but even he got taken for millions by a financial advisor he trusted.

Lesson: Just because someone *says* they're a pro doesn't mean they are. Vet everyone—agents, advisors, accountants. Check licenses. Ask questions. Get second opinions. Don't confuse confidence for credibility.

Mistake #4: Not Paying Taxes

Case Study: Terrell Owens (NFL), Dennis Rodman (NBA), and many others

Plenty of athletes have been hit with massive tax bills and penalties for not filing correctly—or at all.

Lesson: NIL earnings are income. If you get paid and no taxes are taken out, the IRS *still* expects their cut. Always ask:

- "Am I getting a 1099 or W-2?"
- "How much should I be setting aside?"
- "Do I need a CPA?"

If you're making money, **you need a tax plan.**

Mistake #5: Getting Caught in a Social Media Scandal

Case Study: Josh Hader (MLB)

Old tweets surfaced during an All-Star Game, leading to public backlash and brand fallout.

Lesson: What you post now—*even as a teen*—can affect your NIL deals later. Brands drop athletes fast when scandals hit. Be mindful:

- Don't post impulsively
- Avoid offensive or divisive content
- Scrub your past posts regularly
- Don't confuse being "real" with being reckless

Mistake #6: Falling for Scams and Fake Opportunities

Scammers love athletes. Especially young ones with money, followers, or a dream.

Common scams include:

- Fake NIL deals with no contract
- "Brand ambassadors" that make *you* buy product to promote
- Investment pitches from people with no credentials
- Messages that start with "Yo, I can turn your NIL up!" but end with your wallet down

Lesson: If it sounds too good to be true, it probably is. Google the company. Check for reviews. Ask someone you trust. And don't send money to strangers.

Mistake #7: Trying to Take Care of Everybody

This one's emotional. A lot of athletes—especially first-gen earners—feel pressure to provide for everyone. You love your people. You want to help. But...

You can't save everybody. And if you try, you'll drown too.

Lesson: Help when you can, but set boundaries. Create a giving plan or fund if you want to give back. But never let guilt drive your decisions.

Mistake #8: Thinking NIL = Forever

Some athletes get one NIL deal and think it's a long-term bag. Then the brand changes directions. Your performance drops. Or you get injured.

Lesson: NIL is unpredictable. Plan as if it could stop tomorrow. Save, invest, and always have a backup plan. Think: *How can I turn this temporary spotlight into lasting opportunity?*

Checklist: How to Stay Out of Trouble

Read every contract

- Don't make emotional money moves
- Set 20–30% of NIL income aside for taxes and savings

- Keep your circle tight and trustworthy
- Avoid flashy spending traps
- Use social media wisely
- Say NO more than you say YES
- Learn from other people's losses—so you don't repeat them

Final Thoughts: Learn the Lesson Without Living the Loss

The mistakes that cost athletes millions? Most of them were **100% avoidable**.

You're reading this chapter now—*before* the big money hits. That means you already have the advantage. The knowledge. The heads-up.

Now use it.

Because your legacy won't just be about how much you made. It'll be about **how much you kept, how you grew it, and what you built with it.**

Chapter 23: NIL for Women in Sports – Leveling the Playing Field

When NIL became a reality, most people expected male athletes in football and basketball to dominate the spotlight—and in many ways, they have. But here's what no one predicted:

Some of the most powerful NIL brands in the game belong to women.

From gymnasts to hoopers to track stars and even cheerleaders, female athletes are **breaking barriers, redefining influence**, and building NIL empires with strategy, authenticity, and purpose.

This chapter is for the young women turning heads, shifting narratives, and proving you don't have to go pro to profit—you just need the right approach.

Why NIL Is a Game-Changer for Women in Sports

Let's be real—**the sports world hasn't always been equal.**

- Women's sports get less media coverage
- Pro salaries are significantly lower
- Sponsorship dollars often favor men
- And the "marketability" of female athletes is often based on outdated, unfair standards

But NIL flipped the script. Now, your sport, your gender, and your school don't define your worth. *Your story, your brand, and your voice do.*

If you're strategic, **you can compete—and win—on your terms.**

Real Women. Real NIL Wins.

Here are a few standout stories:

- **Livvy Dunne (LSU Gymnastics):** One of the highest-paid female athletes in NIL, blending gymnastics success with a massive social media following and brand alignment.
- **Jada Williams (Basketball):** Built a strong personal brand *before* entering college, showing that NIL starts long before the first game.
- **Haley and Hanna Cavinder (Miami):** Used a combination of social media, business savvy, and NIL rules to cash in on their brand as a twin duo.

Their secret? **Consistency, creativity, and knowing their value.**

You don't need to go viral—you just need to be *intentional.*

Unique Advantages Female Athletes Bring to NIL

Let's flip the narrative—being a woman in this space isn't a disadvantage. It's a superpower. Here's why:

1. Strong Community Engagement

Women athletes tend to build highly loyal, authentic communities—online and offline. Brands *love* that.

2. Versatile Brand Potential

From sports performance to wellness, fashion, education, and advocacy, female athletes often have broader appeal and crossover opportunities.

3. Underserved Market = Untapped Opportunity

Many companies want to support women in sports—but haven't found the right partner yet. Be that partner.

4. Emotional Intelligence & Storytelling
Female athletes often share their journey in deeper, more vulnerable ways—building stronger personal brands and deeper trust with followers.

NIL Challenges Women Still Face

Let's keep it real—there are still hurdles:

- **Judgment about appearance** and "what sells" in the media
- **Unwanted attention** or inappropriate offers
- **Underestimation** from coaches, sponsors, or peers
- **Balancing self-expression** with professionalism

The key is **knowing your worth and setting boundaries**. You don't have to change who you are to be marketable. You just have to be *authentic, focused, and strategic.*

Branding for Impact, Not Just Influence

You don't have to be an influencer to make NIL work. You can build your brand around:

- **Advocacy:** Mental health, equality, education, body positivity
- **Athletic Excellence:** Your grind, stats, records, routines
- **Lifestyle:** Fitness, fashion, faith, cooking, culture
- **Academics:** STEM, business, journalism, public speaking
- **Entrepreneurship:** Launching a product, service, or digital business

Own your narrative. Share your values. Create your own lane.

Keys to Success in the NIL Space as a Woman

Here's your NIL game plan:

1. Know Your Brand

Define your message, values, and tone. Who are you? What do you stand for?

2. Know Your Audience

Who follows you? Who are you trying to inspire, inform, or entertain?

3. Protect Your Image

- Don't sign sketchy contracts
- Avoid brands that don't align with your identity
- Be cautious with how you're portrayed in promotions or media

4. Use Your Platform to Empower Others

Your success isn't just about you. It opens the door for the next generation of girls watching from the stands.

NIL Safety & Boundaries Matter

Women in sports deal with a different kind of attention—and sometimes it crosses the line.

- **Have a separate email for business inquiries**
- **Use a professional agent or rep** to vet deals and contacts
- **Report harassment or inappropriate offers immediately**
- **Take breaks from social media if needed**
- **Don't be afraid to say "No" to deals that feel off**

You don't owe anyone access just because you're visible.

Final Thoughts: You Don't Just Belong—You Lead

NIL is more than money. It's **visibility, voice, and vision.** And women in sports aren't just catching up—they're **setting the pace**.

You are part of something bigger. You're not just changing your life—you're changing what's possible for all the women who come next.

So build your brand. Be intentional. Take the bag—but take the *right* bag. And do it all with pride, poise, and purpose.

Because you're not just a female athlete. **You're a pioneer.**

Chapter 24: Conversations With Your Parents About Money

"Talking about money doesn't divide us—it builds us."

As a student-athlete, you're in a unique position. You may be one of the first in your family to earn a real income while still in college. With NIL opportunities now on the table, you're managing things like branding, taxes, and bank accounts that most people don't deal with until much later in life—if at all.

But here's the thing: your success with money shouldn't be a solo mission. One of the most important moves you can make is to bring your parents or guardians into the conversation. Whether you were raised by a single mom who worked two jobs to keep the lights on or by two parents who modeled responsible financial behavior, having honest and healthy conversations about money can strengthen your path—and theirs.

Why These Conversations Matter

These talks aren't about asking for permission or proving you've got it all figured out. They're about connection, understanding, and creating a shared vision for the future.

- You're building financial habits that could shape your whole life.

- Your parents may be proud, concerned, or unsure how to help.
- You may be in a position to support your family—but you also need support yourself.
- Talking about money eliminates confusion and assumptions on both sides.

Let's Not Make Money Taboo

In many households, money is a sensitive topic. Maybe it was never talked about. Maybe it was a source of stress or tension. But silence doesn't help—it only creates shame or confusion.

Money is just a tool. Talking about it openly can bring clarity and opportunity for everyone involved.

Topics to Talk About With Your Parents

You don't have to cover all these at once. Start small, stay curious, and lead with respect. These conversations are a chance to grow as a family.

1. What Was Money Like Growing Up?

Ask:

- "What did you learn about money when you were younger?"
- "Was money talked about in your home?"
- "Were there things you had to figure out on your own?"

Understanding your parents' background with money can give you context for their values, fears, or habits.

2. What Are Our Family's Financial Goals?

Ask:

- "Are there goals we're working toward as a family?"
- "What would financial peace look like for us?"
- "How can my NIL opportunity support us—not just now, but long-term?"

This helps shift the conversation from short-term help to long-term planning.

3. How Can I Handle My NIL Income the Right Way?

Ask:

- "Can we build a budget together?"
- "Should I open my own bank account?"
- "Can we talk to someone together—like a financial coach or advisor?"

This approach invites your parents to grow with you and builds trust without giving up your independence.

4. What Monthly Bills or Financial Responsibilities Do We Have?

Ask:

- "Can you show me what our expenses look like each month?"
- "How do you manage bills and due dates?"
- "Is there anything I should start taking care of myself?"

When you understand what goes into running a household, you become more financially grounded and prepared.

5. What Should I Know About Credit?

Ask:

- "How did you first learn about credit?"
- "Have you ever had debt you had to overcome?"
- "What should I avoid as I start building my credit score?"

This conversation can prevent future mistakes and build healthy habits early on.

6. Do We Save or Invest? Should I Start?

Ask:

- "What's our approach to saving?"
- "Do we have anything set aside for emergencies?"
- "Would it make sense for me to start saving now or investing for the future?"

Even if your family hasn't saved much, starting this conversation can lead to powerful new habits—for everyone.

7. What Do You Wish You'd Known About Money?

Ask:

- "If you could go back and give your younger self financial advice, what would it be?"
- "What do you wish someone had taught you?"
- "What do you hope I don't have to learn the hard way?"

This question can create the deepest connection—because it's about wisdom, not just numbers.

If You Were Raised by a Single Parent

Let them know you see them.

Say things like:

- "I know you've done so much on your own. I want to be smart with my money to help, not add stress."
- "I'm learning about finances, and I'd love to include you in this process."

This isn't about replacing them—it's about growing together and honoring their sacrifices.

If Both Parents Are Involved and Financially Literate

Use their knowledge. They're one of your greatest assets.

Say things like:

- "You both know a lot about money. Can I show you what I'm learning?"
- "I want to make sure I'm not missing anything in my NIL planning."

You don't have to navigate NIL alone when your support system wants you to win.

Final Word: Talk With Love, Not Ego

This is not about impressing your family or defending your choices—it's about building something better, together.

Your NIL income is a starting point. Your relationship with your family is a foundation.

When you connect the two, you create not just wealth—but legacy.

Let the conversation begin.

Chapter 25: What Is the Market, the Economy, and Everything Else You See on TV?

You've probably heard stuff like:

"The market is crashing!"
"The S&P 500 is on a hot streak!"
"The Fed raised interest rates again!"
"Inflation is out of control!"

If you're like most high school athletes, your first reaction might be:

"Cool. What's that got to do with me?"

Here's the truth: understanding the financial game now—before the money comes in—puts you way ahead of most adults. And guess what? The financial world has a lot in common with sports.

There are teams, stats, winning streaks, injuries, slumps, coaches, rules, and momentum shifts.

Once you learn how the game works, you can start *playing to win*—and that starts here.

What Is the Stock Market?

The stock market is where people buy and sell *ownership* in companies. When you buy a stock, you're buying a tiny slice of a company—like Nike, Apple, or Amazon.

Sports analogy:

It's like being part of a team's ownership group. You're not just a fan in the stands—you own a piece. When that team (or company) wins, your share becomes more valuable.

Why Does the Market Go Up or Down?

It all comes down to supply and demand.

If more people want to *buy* a stock, the price goes up.

If more people want to *sell*, the price goes down.

What changes that demand?

News, performance reports, political drama, inflation, interest rates—even tweets.

Sports analogy:

It's like player hype. If a player is dropping 30 points a game, their "value" goes up. If they get injured or start missing games, fans (and investors) start selling.

What's the Difference Between the Stock Market and the Economy?

The stock market is the scoreboard. The economy is the game.

They're connected—but not always the same.

Sports analogy:

The market is like fantasy football. The economy is the real game. Sometimes the stats match up... sometimes they don't.

Is the Market Risky?

Yes—but it's less risky when you're smart.

If you put all your money in one company and it crashes, you lose big.

But if you spread your money across lots of companies—through index funds or ETFs—you protect yourself.

Sports analogy:

One player might get injured. But if you've built a deep team, you're still in the game.

How Should I Start Investing?

Here's the smart playbook:

- Use index funds or ETFs (they include hundreds of companies)
- Open a Roth IRA or brokerage account when you're eligible
- Think long-term
- Stay consistent—even during slumps

Sports analogy:

You don't need fancy plays. Just run the offense, follow the system, and play smart basketball.

When's the Best Time to Start?

Now. Always now.

The earlier you start, the more your money can grow.

Sports analogy:

Champions don't wait for the playoffs to train. They build in the offseason. Start early, and your financial game will be strong by the time it counts.

What's the S&P 500?

It's a list of the 500 biggest companies in the U.S. Investors use it to track how the market is doing overall.

Sports analogy:

It's like the national rankings. If most of the Top 25 are winning, the league looks strong.

What's a Bull Market vs. a Bear Market?

- **Bull market:** Prices going up, confidence is high
- **Bear market:** Prices dropping, people are panicking

Sports analogy:

A bull market is a winning streak. A bear market is a slump. Stay calm through both.

Should I Sell When the Market Drops?

No. That locks in your losses.

Sports analogy:

You don't bench your star player after one bad game. You trust the process and ride it out.

How Much Money Do I Need to Start?

Not much. Some apps let you start with as little as $5–$50.

Sports analogy:

You don't have to be the MVP on day one. Just get on the team, show up, and do the reps.

Can I Make Fast Money?

Yes, but it's risky.

Day trading = gambling.

Investing = building.

Sports analogy:

Anyone can hit a half-court buzzer beater once. Champions win with consistent free throws, solid defense, and smart plays.

What's an ETF?

An ETF (Exchange-Traded Fund) is a bundle of investments you can buy like one stock. It's like owning a little bit of a whole bunch of companies.

Sports analogy:

It's like drafting an entire all-star team with one pick.

Is Investing Only for Rich People?

Nope.

Investing is for *anyone* who wants to build wealth. You don't need to start big. You just need to *start.*

Sports analogy:

Great careers start in high school gyms, not NBA arenas. The work you put in now matters.

Stocks vs. Bonds – What's the Difference?

- **Stock = Ownership** in a company (can grow fast, but risky)
- **Bond = Loan** to a company or government (steadier, slower growth)

Sports analogy:

Stocks are like star scorers. Bonds are the quiet defenders. You need both.

What's Diversification?

It means spreading your money out—not putting it all in one place.

Sports analogy:

You don't build a team with only point guards. You need shooters, size, speed, defense.

Why Do People Say "Buy Low, Sell High"?

That's how you profit. But most people panic and do the opposite.

Sports analogy:

You don't trade your best player when they're in a slump. You trust they'll bounce back.

What Should I Invest In?

Start with:

- S&P 500 index funds
- Total Market ETFs
- Low-cost options
- Reinvest your dividends
- Think long-term

Sports analogy:

You don't have to hit threes all game. Take high-percentage shots. Stick to your system.

What Happens in a Recession?

A recession is when the economy slows down. People spend less. Jobs are cut. Companies pull back.

The market might drop—but it usually recovers.

Sports analogy:
A recession is a rebuilding season. It's tough—but you use it to grow and prepare for the next big run.

Do I Need a Financial Advisor?

Not at first. Use apps like:

- Fidelity
- Vanguard
- Schwab
- Public
- M1 Finance
- Betterment

As your NIL income grows, a financial advisor can be your coach—helping you design plays for the future.

What's the #1 Rule of Investing?

Start early. Stay consistent. Don't panic.
Sports analogy:
Great players aren't always flashy—but they're dependable. They show up, follow the plan, and stay focused.

What's a Dividend?

A dividend is a bonus some companies give to their shareholders—just for owning stock.
Sports analogy:
It's like getting paid even when you're on the bench. You're still part of the squad.

How Often Should I Check My Investments?

Not every day. Maybe once a month. Maybe once a quarter.

Sports analogy:

You don't stare at the scoreboard during warm-ups. Focus on the game. Stats come later.

What's a Stock Split?

When a stock's price gets too high, the company splits it to make it more affordable. You still own the same total value—just more shares.

Sports analogy:

It's like changing jersey numbers. The look changes, but the role stays the same.

What's a Market Correction?

When the market drops 10% from a recent high, that's a correction. It's normal. It's healthy.

Sports analogy:

It's like a timeout after a sloppy quarter—not a meltdown. Just time to reset.

Should I Invest if the Market Is Going Down?

Yes. That's often the best time. Prices are lower, and you're getting value.

Sports analogy:

It's like buying your favorite kicks at 30% off. Still the same gear—just cheaper.

Can I Lose All My Money?

If you invest in just one stock? Yes.

If you diversify with ETFs or index funds? Very unlikely.

Sports analogy:

One player might get injured. But with a strong bench, you're still in the game.

Mutual Fund vs. ETF?

Both hold baskets of investments.

- **Mutual fund**: Trades once per day, may have higher fees
- **ETF**: Trades like a stock all day, usually cheaper

Sports analogy:

Mutual funds are like old-school coaches—reliable but slow. ETFs are the modern system—efficient and flexible.

What Are Interest Rates?

Interest rates = cost of borrowing money.

When the Fed raises rates, it makes borrowing more expensive. That slows down spending—and can cause markets to drop.

Sports analogy:

It's like when your coach makes you run extra sprints. Slows you down short-term, but builds long-term stamina.

What's Dollar-Cost Averaging?

It means investing the same amount of money regularly—no matter what the market is doing.

Example:

$100/month into a fund. When prices are low, you buy more. When prices are high, you buy less. It evens out.

Sports analogy:

It's like showing up to practice every week. Doesn't matter if you're tired or on fire—the consistency builds greatness.

Final Thoughts: Learn the Game. Play It Smart. Build Your Legacy.

The stock market isn't just for grownups or rich people. It's for you—right now.

Investing is a long game. And just like sports, it rewards discipline, patience, and reps.

Build a team of smart investments. Diversify your roster. Train consistently. Don't panic in the tough moments. Don't get cocky in the wins.

Start small. Stay focused.

Play for your future—not just for the moment.

Because real legacy?

It isn't just earned under the lights.

It's built in the background, with smart money moves that compound over time.

You're already an athlete. Now it's time to think like an investor too.

Chapter 26: Helping Without Hurting – How to Support Loved Ones Without Going Broke

You Love Them. But You Can't Save Them All.

Let's talk about one of the hardest parts of coming into money—especially NIL money when you're young and the first in your family to earn like this.

Helping a single mom who's always held it down? You want to.

Helping your dad who's always struggled but showed up for your games? Feels like the least you can do.

Supporting a friend who's stuck or down bad? They were with you before the spotlight.

You want to be loyal. You want to be generous. You don't want to seem selfish.

But if you're not careful, you'll **drown while trying to save everyone else**.

This chapter is about doing it differently. About **helping without hurting**. About giving with **boundaries**, not guilt. About building a future where you don't have to say, "I used to have money..."

Start With This Truth: You're Not Their Retirement Plan

If you're earning NIL money and you're the first in the family to "make it," people will look to you for support. Sometimes it's asked for. Sometimes it's expected silently. Either way, you need a plan before you get pulled into financial chaos.

You are not your family's emergency fund.

You are not the government.

You are not a bottomless pit of money.

Even if you choose to help—**it has to be structured**.

Option 1: The Monthly Budget Strategy

Let's say you want to help Mom with groceries, bills, or rent. Instead of saying "yes" every time she calls, you set a **monthly family support budget.**

Example:

You decide $500 a month is what you can afford to help with **consistently** without sacrificing your own savings, investments, or goals.

Here's how that looks:

- $200 goes toward groceries or utilities
- $200 is paid directly to her landlord or mortgage company
- $100 goes on a pre-loaded debit card for other needs

Once you hit that $500 for the month, **you're done.**

If someone asks for more?

You say:

> *"I already hit my family support budget for the month. We can revisit it next month, but I can't go over that."*

You're not being cold—you're sticking to your boundaries.

Option 2: The Lump Sum Strategy

Maybe you don't want to deal with monthly requests. Maybe you want to give a little breathing room up front.

That's when you decide to **give a one-time gift**, and that's it.

Example:

You get a $20,000 NIL deal. You decide you can spare $2,000 to help Mom with overdue bills or car repairs.

You say:

> *"This is a one-time gift. I love you and wanted to do something meaningful. But after this, I won't be able to give more right now."*

Then you send it. You don't revisit. You don't fall into guilt. You protect your plan.

And here's the most important part: **you don't keep reloading the gift.**

This isn't a subscription service. It's one-time support—done with love and limits.

If It's More Than One Person...

What if you're trying to help your mom *and* your dad *and* your siblings *and* your childhood best friend who's "just tryna get back on their feet"?

Same rules. Set a **total monthly or annual support budget**, and divide it—if you want.

Example: You decide to budget $6,000 for family/friend support per year. That's $500/month total.

- Mom gets $300
- Dad gets $100
- Your best friend gets $100

That's it.

You don't add more. You don't loan more. You don't get drawn into guilt.

If one person's situation changes, it doesn't automatically mean your budget does.

Your **financial plan comes first**. Everyone else fits within that plan—or not at all.

Say It Early, Say It Often

If you don't say **how** and **how much** you're willing to help, people will assume it's unlimited. And assumptions are where resentment and entitlement grow.

Have the conversation. It might be awkward, but it's worth it.

You say:

> *"I love you, and I'm proud to be in a place to help. But I'm setting a boundary. I've got a budget for support, and once I hit that number, I can't go past it. It's not personal—it's me protecting my future."*

And when they say "but just this one time..."

You hold the line.

How to Avoid Enabling

Helping becomes **enabling** when:

- They stop trying to help themselves
- They start expecting it
- They guilt you when you say no
- You give money that solves the same problem over and over again
- You feel resentment instead of peace

To avoid enabling, try this:

- Pay the bill directly, don't give cash
- Offer help with job searching, not just money
- Suggest financial literacy resources
- Make the help temporary, not open-ended

If they need $200 for rent every month, what they really need is a plan, not a handout. You can love someone without being their financial crutch.

If They Get Mad, That's Okay

Boundaries make people uncomfortable—especially if they're used to you saying "yes."

They may accuse you of changing.

They may say, "You forgot where you came from."

They may try guilt or shame.

Let them.

Because the goal isn't to win everyone's approval.

The goal is to build something that lasts—for you and for the people you'll be able to help down the line **the right way**.

You can't pour into others if your own cup is empty.

Final Thoughts: Help With Strategy, Not Emotion

You're not heartless for saying no.

You're not selfish for setting limits.

You're not wrong for wanting to keep what you earned.

If you *choose* to help family or friends, do it:

- With intention
- With a clear budget
- With hard boundaries
- Without shame

Because the best gift you can give isn't a check.

It's the example of financial strength, discipline, and long-term thinking.

If they love you, they'll understand.

And if they don't now… they will when you're still standing strong ten years from now while others are broke and bitter.

That's real love. That's real leadership. That's legacy.

Chapter 27: The Power of No – Protecting Your Peace and Your Pockets

Introduction: When the Checks Start Coming In, So Do the Requests

When the NIL money starts flowing, it's exciting. You're signing endorsement deals, making money through content, merchandise, appearances, and sponsorships. But just as real as the income is the pressure. The calls and texts start coming in. Family members you love ask for "just a little help." Friends expect you to cover dinner, buy gear, or invest in their "big idea." Old contacts come out of nowhere with financial needs or business pitches.

Saying "no" in these moments isn't being cold—it's being smart. It's not just about protecting money, it's about protecting your future, your mental health, and your peace of mind. This chapter will help you learn how to say no clearly, kindly, and confidently—without guilt.

Why It's Hard to Say "No"

Let's start with the truth: for many student-athletes, especially first-generation wealth earners, success isn't seen as just personal—it's a win for the entire family. It can feel like everyone is depending on you. Maybe you:

- Feel like the "chosen one" expected to lift everyone up
- Want to give back out of gratitude
- Feel guilty for having something others don't
- Think people won't understand if you say no

These emotions are valid. But always saying yes—especially when you can't afford to—doesn't help anyone in the long run. You didn't work hard just to become someone else's safety net. You worked hard to build a life of freedom and opportunity. Protect that.

The Real Cost of Always Saying Yes

Handing out money feels good in the short term. You feel generous. You feel needed. You feel like you're doing right by people who matter to you. But here's what often happens over time:

- Your finances start slipping—savings disappear, bills pile up, and you fall behind on your own goals.
- People get used to the handouts. What felt like help becomes an expectation.
- You find it hard to say no later. And when you finally do, people react negatively.
- Resentment grows. You feel used, and they feel entitled.

Always saying yes creates a pattern. You stop investing in yourself. You become the plan for everyone else. But who is helping you?

What to Say Instead of "No"

Saying "no" doesn't have to be rude or aggressive. You can communicate boundaries with kindness, clarity, and firmness. Here are some ways to say no—without feeling like a bad person:

- "I've already committed my money to a financial plan. Everything's accounted for."
- "I'm trying to build something that lasts. I can't give out money right now."
- "I've talked with my advisor, and right now I'm not in a position to help."
- "I love you, but I'm not loaning or gifting money to anyone right now."
- "I can't give you money, but I'm happy to support you in other ways."

Here's a tip: blame the plan, not the person. Instead of making it about their request being unreasonable, make it about your plan being the priority. You aren't rejecting them—you're sticking to your structure.

Enabling vs. Empowering

Let's say you help someone out. Maybe you pay a car note or cover rent one month. It feels good. But what happens next month? And the month after that?

If you give money without teaching financial skills, you're not helping—you're enabling. That means you're creating a dependency. Now, instead of solving a problem, you've just delayed it and trained someone to come to you again.

Empowering someone is different. It looks like:

- Helping them get a job or build a budget
- Encouraging them to learn about money
- Offering guidance instead of a handout
- Supporting their growth, not just their survival

Handouts end. Education multiplies.

You Are Not Their Financial Plan

If someone's entire financial recovery depends on *you*, that's a problem. You are not their emergency fund, retirement plan, or financial institution.

Here are some boundaries that protect you:

- No loans, no exceptions
- No gifts unless it's budgeted and doesn't hurt you
- No investing in someone else's business without full due diligence
- No cosigning or opening credit in your name for anyone

If you decide to help, do it intentionally and once—not habitually and out of guilt.

Legacy Over Likes

A lot of athletes fall into the trap of being liked. They want to be seen as generous, successful, and loyal. But being liked by everyone can leave you broke. What matters more than likes is legacy.

Legacy is what you leave behind—wealth, wisdom, and example. Protecting your money now means being able to:

- Buy your first home
- Invest in a business of your own
- Support your future kids
- Take care of your parents in retirement
- Give back to your community in bigger ways later

Saying no today might hurt someone's feelings. But saying yes and ending up broke helps no one.

When You're the First to Make It

Being the first in your family or community to have money is a beautiful but heavy role. You feel the pressure to give back. You feel the eyes on you. You feel like if you don't help, no one will.

But remember:

- You help people best when you're stable yourself.
- You can't give from an empty account.
- Just because you're first doesn't mean you're responsible for everyone else's success.

You can inspire others by showing what responsible money looks like. That example is worth more than any handout.

Boundaries Are Not Betrayal

Let's get something straight: saying no is not betrayal. It's self-respect. Setting boundaries doesn't make you cold, distant, or selfish. It means you know where your limits are.

Saying no now may mean fewer calls, fewer messages, or some awkward silence. That's okay. People who love you will understand. And if they don't, that tells you something too.

Boundaries protect your ability to keep showing up—for yourself, and one day, for others who *truly* need it.

Create a Script

Don't wait until you're put on the spot. Have a go-to response ready for when people ask for money.

Here's a script:

"I've created a financial plan for my income, and I'm not giving out any money right now. I hope you understand. I'm focused on building something long-term."

Or:

"I've made the decision not to lend or give money to friends or family. It's a personal boundary I'm holding to make sure I stay on track."

You can adjust the tone based on who you're talking to—but keep the boundary firm.

Help Without Giving Money

Sometimes you want to help—but not with cash. That's a great instinct. Here's how you can still be supportive:

- Recommend a job lead or resource
- Help someone budget or apply for assistance
- Introduce them to a mentor or advisor
- Give them books or podcasts on financial literacy
- Offer your time or emotional support instead

Money isn't the only way to care.

If You Do Say Yes, Do It Right

If you decide to help someone financially, set clear terms:

- Be specific about the amount
- Make it a one-time gift, not a recurring expectation
- If it's a loan, write it down and agree on a repayment timeline
- Say, "This is a one-time thing," and stick to it

Helping someone once doesn't mean you're now responsible for them. Be generous on your terms—not theirs.

Know the Red Flags

Some people won't take no for an answer. Watch for:

- Guilt-tripping: "But you owe me after everything I did for you."
- Pressure: "You have the money, why not help?"
- Repeated asks: "Just this one more time..."
- Manipulation: "If you really loved me, you'd do this."

These are signs someone may be more interested in your money than your well-being. Don't fall for it.

What Happens If You Don't Learn to Say No

Many athletes give and give—until there's nothing left.

They sign great deals, but they never build anything for themselves.

They support everyone except the one person who earned it: themselves.

Then the deals dry up. The attention fades. And the money's gone.

And suddenly, all the people who were always around... disappear.

Learn to say no now, so that when the spotlight dims, you're still standing on something solid.

Closing Thoughts: Say No Now, So You Can Say Yes Later

Saying no today protects your ability to say yes tomorrow.

Yes to a house.

Yes to investing.

Yes to giving generously—when you're in a place to do it.

Yes to building real wealth.

Yes to your own dreams.

Don't let short-term pressure ruin your long-term vision. You are not just someone's ATM. You are a brand, a business, and a future success story in the making.

Protect your peace. Guard your generosity. Lead with wisdom.
And always remember: *"No" is a complete sentence.*

Chapter 28: The Eighth Wonder of the World – Understanding Compound Interest

Introduction: Why Time Is the Most Powerful Asset You Have

When it comes to building wealth, most people think it takes a lot of money. But the truth is, it takes **time and consistency** more than anything else. One of the most powerful forces in all of finance is **compound interest**—and the earlier you start using it, the more it works in your favor.

Albert Einstein allegedly called compound interest the "eighth wonder of the world." He supposedly said:

> *"He who understands it, earns it. He who doesn't, pays it."*

Whether or not Einstein actually said it doesn't matter—because the principle is *absolutely* true. Compound interest can make your NIL money grow exponentially over time, or it can work against you if you're borrowing and building debt.

In this chapter, you'll learn what compound interest is, how it works, how to make it your financial superpower, and how to avoid being crushed by it through credit cards, loans, or missed opportunities.

What Is Compound Interest?

Compound interest is interest that earns interest. You make money not just on your original investment (called the "principal"), but also on the interest that investment earns over time.

Unlike simple interest, which only pays on the principal, compound interest grows faster and faster over time because every year, you're earning interest on a bigger number.

It's like a snowball rolling downhill—slow at first, but eventually unstoppable.

Example:

If you invest $1,000 at 10% annual interest:

- **Year 1**: You earn $100. Now you have $1,100.
- **Year 2**: You earn $110 (10% of $1,100). Now you have $1,210.
- **Year 3**: You earn $121. Now you have $1,331.

Over time, the gains get bigger—not because you added more money, but because the growth builds on itself.

Why Compound Interest Matters for You (Especially Now)

You have something most people don't: **youth**. And when it comes to compound interest, the earlier you start, the more powerful it becomes.

Even small amounts can turn into huge sums if you give them time.

Let's compare two athletes:

- **Athlete A** starts investing $200/month at age 18 and stops at age 28. She invests for just 10 years—$24,000 total.
- **Athlete B** waits until age 28 to start and invests $200/month until age 65. He invests for 37 years—$88,800 total.

Assuming an 8% return, who ends up with more money at 65?

Answer: Athlete A, who started earlier, ends up with more money—*even though she invested for fewer years and less money*—because her money had more time to grow.

Time Is More Valuable Than Timing

A lot of people try to "time the market." They wait for the right moment to invest. But when it comes to compound interest, time **in** the market matters far more than trying to time the market.

The best time to start was yesterday. The second-best time is today.

The longer your money stays invested, the more compound interest can do its magic.

Rule of 72 – The Shortcut to Doubling Your Money

Want to know how long it takes to double your money with compound interest? Use the **Rule of 72**.

Just divide 72 by your expected annual return.

For example:

- 72 ÷ 6% = 12 years to double
- 72 ÷ 9% = 8 years to double
- 72 ÷ 12% = 6 years to double

So if you earn 9% annually, your money will double about every 8 years. That means $10,000 becomes $20,000 in 8 years… $40,000 in 16 years… and $80,000 in 24 years. Without you adding a single extra dollar.

The Compounding Timeline – Why Waiting Hurts

Here's the key: **every year you wait makes it harder to catch up.** Let's look at three athletes who all invest $100/month at 8% return.

- **Start at age 18**: $100/month = ~$351,428 by age 65
- **Start at age 28**: ~$164,870 by age 65
- **Start at age 38**: ~$74,336 by age 65

Waiting just 10 years can cost you hundreds of thousands of dollars. That's the power of compound interest. It rewards early starters and punishes procrastinators.

Where Can You Use Compound Interest?

You don't need to be a Wall Street trader to benefit from compounding. Here are common accounts that allow compound interest to work for you:

- **Roth IRA** – Tax-free growth and withdrawals in retirement
- **Traditional IRA or 401(k)** – Tax-deferred growth
- **High-yield savings accounts** – Low growth, but still compound
- **Investment accounts (brokerage accounts)** – Stocks, ETFs, mutual funds
- **HSA (Health Savings Account)** – Triple tax benefit if used properly

Start small. Stay consistent. Let time do the heavy lifting.

Compound Interest Can Hurt You Too

So far we've talked about compound interest working *for* you. But it can also work *against* you—especially when you're dealing with **debt**.

Credit cards, payday loans, and high-interest loans compound your **debt**, not your wealth.

Let's say you owe $5,000 on a credit card at 22% interest. If you don't pay it off quickly, that balance can balloon. You end up paying thousands more than you borrowed.

The same snowball effect that makes investments grow can turn debt into a financial disaster.

Protect Yourself: Avoid the Trap of Reverse Compounding

To make compound interest work for you, not against you:

- **Pay off credit cards** in full each month
- **Avoid payday loans** or high-interest borrowing
- **Don't finance things you don't need**
- **Invest early and regularly**—even small amounts matter
- **Automate savings and investment** to stay consistent

The goal is to **earn** compound interest, not **owe** it.

The Mindset Shift: Think Like an Investor, Not a Spender

Here's the bottom line: when you get NIL money, you'll be tempted to **spend it**. That's natural. But every dollar you spend today is a dollar that won't grow tomorrow.

Think like an investor. Ask:

- Will this help me grow long-term?
- Am I giving this dollar a job, or am I letting it disappear?
- Can I invest this now so I don't have to work as hard later?

Compound interest is like planting a tree. You won't get shade immediately—but in a few years, you'll be thankful you did.

How to Get Started – Action Steps

1. **Open a Roth IRA** – It's tax-free growth, and you can contribute up to $6,500/year (as of 2025) if you have earned income.
2. **Set up recurring contributions** – Automate $50, $100, or more monthly.
3. **Choose a low-cost index fund** – S&P 500 or Total Market index funds are great for starters.
4. **Leave it alone** – Resist the urge to withdraw. Let it compound.
5. **Check once a year** – Rebalance if needed, but don't obsess.
6. **Increase contributions as your income grows** – Pay yourself first.

Final Thoughts: Make Compound Interest Your Teammate

As a student-athlete, you understand what it means to play the long game. You show up, you train, and the results come later. Compound interest works the same way.

It rewards patience, discipline, and consistency.

The money you invest now has the power to buy your freedom later—freedom to choose your job, support your family, travel, give back, and retire early.

So don't just hustle for NIL money today. **Put some of it to work for the future you.**

Compound interest doesn't need you to be rich to start.

It just needs you to start.

Chapter 29: Wrong Examples

Here are several **real-world examples of athletes who made millions and then lost it all (or most of it)** due to poor financial decisions, lack of guidance, or unsustainable lifestyles. These stories can serve as powerful teaching tools in your book or workshops to show the importance of planning, saying "no," and building wealth the right way.

1. Allen Iverson – NBA

Estimated career earnings: Over $200 million

What happened: Lavish spending, generosity to friends and family, and a divorce drained his bank account. He was known for flying his crew on private jets, buying dozens of cars, and spending tens of thousands at a time in malls. He once reportedly refused to fly commercial—even for one night.

How he bounced back: Fortunately, Reebok had a **$32 million trust** set aside for him that he can access at age 55. That move likely saved his financial future.

2. Antoine Walker – NBA

Estimated career earnings: $108 million

What happened: Walker invested in failed real estate deals, supported over 70 friends and family members, and lived a high-spending lifestyle with luxury cars, jewelry, and gambling. He filed for bankruptcy just two years after retiring.

Lesson: Even $100 million isn't enough if you don't set boundaries and manage wisely.

3. Vince Young – NFL

Estimated career earnings: Around $35 million

What happened: Young famously spent $5,000 a week at The Cheesecake Factory and once bought every seat on a Southwest Airlines flight—just so he could fly alone. He trusted the wrong people, didn't track spending, and filed for bankruptcy in 2014.

4. Delonte West – NBA

Estimated career earnings: $16 million

What happened: After a solid NBA career, West faced mental health struggles and poor financial decisions. At one point, he was seen homeless and panhandling. His story is heartbreaking and reminds us that financial literacy and mental health go hand in hand.

Current status: With support from former teammate Mark Cuban, West entered rehab and has been working to rebuild his life.

5. Bernie Kosar – NFL

Estimated career earnings: Over $20 million

What happened: Kosar tried to help too many people. He once said he had **60 checking accounts** and over **50 real estate partnerships**, most of which failed. He gave away money without structure and later filed for bankruptcy.

Lesson: You can't save everyone. If you're everyone's emergency fund, you'll go broke trying to play hero.

6. Lenny Dykstra – MLB

Estimated career earnings: $36 million

What happened: After retirement, Dykstra lived lavishly and pursued risky business ventures with borrowed money. He declared bankruptcy in 2009 and was later sentenced to prison for bankruptcy fraud and money laundering.

Lesson: Taking financial risks without a plan can cost you more than just money—it can take your freedom.

7. Mike Tyson – Boxing

Estimated career earnings: $400+ million

What happened: Lavish spending on mansions, exotic animals (he once owned three Bengal tigers), luxury cars, and a massive entourage led Tyson to bankruptcy in 2003. He admitted to spending **$1 million per month at one point**.

Current status: Tyson has made a successful comeback through podcasting, entertainment, and cannabis ventures.

Lesson: It's not about how much you make—it's how much you keep.

8. JaMarcus Russell – NFL

Estimated career earnings: $40 million

What happened: Russell signed one of the biggest rookie contracts in NFL history but had little structure or financial discipline. He reportedly spent heavily on jewelry, cars, and poor investments. He never became a consistent starter, and his money didn't last.

Lesson: Earning potential doesn't matter if you don't have a financial game plan.

9. Sheryl Swoopes – WNBA

Estimated career earnings: Millions through salary and endorsements

What happened: Despite being a pioneer in women's basketball, Swoopes filed for bankruptcy in 2004. She made poor investment decisions, including trusting the wrong advisors and business ventures that failed.

Lesson: Even trailblazers need financial education and trusted guidance.

10. Evander Holyfield – Boxing

Estimated career earnings: Over $200 million

What happened: Holyfield bought a 109-room mansion, fathered 11 children with multiple women (with huge child support obligations), and had extravagant spending habits. He lost his home to foreclosure and faced serious financial setbacks.

Lesson: Lifestyle inflation and unchecked generosity can drain even the biggest bank accounts.

Final Thoughts

These examples aren't just cautionary tales—they're reminders of how fast money can disappear without a plan. Whether you're earning $10K or $10 million from NIL deals, you need:

- A budget
- A plan
- Financial boundaries
- Trusted advisors
- A long-term mindset

Learn from their mistakes—so your story can be one of legacy, not loss.

Chapter 30: What's a Portfolio? Build Your Game Plan, Diversify Your Lineup

Every Athlete Needs a Game Plan

Think of your financial future like a championship season. You wouldn't hit the court or field without a playbook, right? You need strategy. You need roles. You need a team that can win in different situations.

That's exactly what a **portfolio** is. It's your financial lineup. It's a mix of different players—investments—each with their own strengths, risks, and jobs to do. When you build a smart portfolio, you're giving yourself the best shot at long-term success.

So, What's in a Portfolio?

A portfolio is your mix of money moves. It includes things like:

- Stocks (your offensive players – high-scoring, high-risk)
- Bonds (your defense – stable, dependable, protects the lead)
- Cash (your bench – ready when you need quick subs or timeouts)
- Real estate, ETFs, mutual funds (your utility players – all-around options)

Just like you wouldn't play a whole basketball game with only point guards, you don't want your financial team made up of one type of investment.

You need balance. You need different players. That's where **diversification** comes in.

Why Diversification Is Like Having a Strong Team

If you put your entire financial future into one stock or one type of investment, it's like betting the whole season on one player. What if they get injured? What if they have a bad game? You're cooked.

Diversification is spreading out your risk. It's like building a full roster—scorers, defenders, role players—so if one guy has a bad night, others can step up.

When the market gets rough (and it will), your diversified portfolio helps you stay in the game.

Different Portfolio "Teams" – Conservative, Moderate, Aggressive

Depending on your goals, age, and mindset, you're going to want a different type of portfolio "team." Let's break it down.

Conservative Portfolio – Play Defense First

This is the type of lineup you build when protecting the lead matters more than running up the score.

You're stacking your team with safe, slow-moving players: mostly bonds, with a few stocks sprinkled in.

It's like playing zone defense, controlling the tempo, limiting fast breaks. You're not trying to blow anyone out—you're just trying not to lose.

Who's it for?

- Athletes close to retirement

- People who need their money soon
- Anyone with a low risk tolerance

Pros:

- Less volatile
- Easier to sleep at night
- Steady, predictable returns

Cons:

- Less upside
- May not beat inflation
- Not ideal for young players building wealth

Moderate Portfolio – Balanced Offense and Defense

This is your two-way team. A good mix of offense (stocks) and defense (bonds).

You've got players who can score, but you're not ignoring protection. It's like a team that can grind out close games and still run when they need to.

Who's it for?

- Athletes with 5–10 year goals
- Those who want growth but hate chaos
- Anyone building wealth and playing it smart

Pros:

- Balanced risk and return
- Can handle market swings better
- Suitable for most people in the middle of their career

Cons:

- Can feel slow when the market's hot
- Still risky in downturns
- Requires patience

Aggressive Portfolio – Go For the Win

This is your fast-paced, high-scoring team. Mostly made up of stocks, it's built to run the floor, attack constantly, and take big swings.

It's not for the faint of heart—but over time, this strategy usually puts the most points on the board.

Who's it for?

- Young athletes
- People who won't need their money for 10+ years
- Risk-takers who understand the long game

Pros:

- Huge upside potential
- Great for early wealth building
- Takes full advantage of compounding over time

Cons:

- Big mood swings (a.k.a. market drops)
- Emotionally tough to stick with
- Not for short-term goals

How to Choose Your Strategy – When to Attack, When to Hold Back

Just like in sports, you change your game plan depending on the situation. You don't full-court press up 30 points in the fourth quarter. You don't play conservative if you're down 10 with two minutes left.

Same with investing.

Be more aggressive when:

- You're in your 20s and 30s
- You don't need the money for at least 10 years
- You're focused on building, not protecting
- You can handle the emotional swings of the market

Be more conservative when:

- You're close to needing the money (within 5 years)
- You're about to retire
- You're risk-averse and losing money keeps you up at night
- You've already won financially and just want to protect your lead

Your Portfolio Changes With Your Season

Your investing strategy should evolve just like your athletic career.

Early in your career? You're trying to grow, build, and take some smart risks. That's your aggressive portfolio phase.

Mid-career? You're balancing growth with protection. That's your moderate stage.

Later in life? You've built your lead—now it's about not blowing it. That's when you go conservative.

The key is to know where you are in the game and adjust your lineup accordingly.

Final Thoughts – Build a Dynasty, Not a One-Season Wonder

A good coach knows it's not just about winning one game—it's about building a program that lasts. Your portfolio is your program.

Don't get distracted by hype plays. Don't panic during a losing streak. Don't chase risky trades just because someone else hit big.

Stick to the fundamentals:

- Diversify your roster
- Match your strategy to your season
- Adjust over time
- Play the long game

Because when you look back after 10, 20, 30 years... you'll be glad you didn't go for just highlight reels. You built something solid.

You didn't just play the game.

You *owned* the league.

Chapter 31: How to Start Investing – Your NIL Playbook for Building Wealth

Don't Just Get Paid. Build Something With It.

So you just landed your first NIL deal. Maybe it's $1,000. Maybe it's $10,000. Maybe more.

The first thought? Celebrate.

Buy some new gear. Take a trip. Post it all on the 'Gram.

We get it. And hey—enjoy a little bit. You earned it.

But if you want to do what pros do—the *real* flex is this:

Build something that lasts.

Because the truth is, money comes fast... and goes even faster. Unless you make a plan.

This chapter is about *what to do next*—how to grow your money, protect your money, and make smart moves with your NIL income so that your first check becomes your *first step* toward long-term wealth.

Step 1: What Does It Mean to Invest?

Investing is how you turn your money into *more* money.

Instead of letting your cash sit in a checking account (or spending it all), you put it into things that can grow in value over time—like stocks, bonds, or funds.

The more consistently you invest, the more your money builds on itself.

That's called **compound interest**, and it's one of the most powerful tools in the financial world.

Step 2: Know What You're Investing For

Before you invest a dime, ask yourself:

- When will I need this money?
- Am I okay with it going up and down in value sometimes?
- Am I saving for short-term goals (like a car or tuition), or for the long haul?

If you won't need the money for at least 5 years, investing makes sense.

If you need it sooner? Keep that part in cash.

Step 3: Picking the Right Kind of Account

There are different ways to invest—and the type of account you use matters, especially for taxes. Here's a quick breakdown:

Roth IRA

- Grows **tax-free**
- You can withdraw your money in retirement with no taxes
- You must have **earned income** to contribute
- Limit: $6,500/year (as of 2025)

Why it's great for young athletes:

You're likely in a low tax bracket now, so paying taxes upfront means you never pay again on that money—ever.

Traditional IRA

- May give you a **tax break now**
- You pay taxes later when you withdraw
- Same yearly contribution limit
- May not be available to everyone based on income

Taxable Brokerage Account

- No income or contribution limits
- Pay taxes on your earnings
- Super flexible—you can withdraw money anytime

Best for: Any extra cash you want to invest *beyond* your Roth IRA limit or for medium-term goals.

SEP IRA or SIMPLE IRA

These are for entrepreneurs and people running businesses—so if you set up your own NIL brand or LLC, these might apply to you down the line.

Step 4: What If You Got a $100,000 NIL Check?

Let's break it down. Here's how a smart athlete handles that kind of payday:

First: Set Aside Taxes

NIL money isn't tax-free. If taxes aren't being withheld, you need to save about 30%.

- **$100,000 x 30% = $30,000 for taxes**
- Put that money in a separate account. Don't touch it.

Next: Fund a Roth IRA

If you're eligible, this is a no-brainer.

- **Max: $6,500 into a Roth IRA**
- Invest it in something like an S&P 500 index fund and let it grow tax-free.

Invest More in a Brokerage Account

Still got money left? Great—keep building.

- **Put $30,000–$40,000 into a taxable account**
- Pick low-cost index funds. Don't overthink it.

Keep Some in Cash

Things happen. NIL can be unpredictable.

- **Set aside $10,000–$15,000 for emergencies**
- Use a high-yield savings account so it earns a little while it waits.

Reward Yourself (Within Reason)

Enjoy a slice of the win.

- **Spend $5,000–$10,000 guilt-free**
- But put a cap on it. Be smart. Don't blow the bag.

Your $100K Game Plan:

- $30,000 → Taxes
- $6,500 → Roth IRA
- $35,000 → Brokerage account
- $15,000 → Cash savings
- $8,500 → Enjoyment

Step 5: Keep It Going

Even if you're not getting a six-figure deal yet, the *system stays the same*:

- Save for taxes
- Invest what you can
- Build a cushion
- Spend what's left—intentionally
- Repeat

Set up automatic transfers. Stick to simple investments (like ETFs). Let time and discipline do the work.

Final Thoughts: Don't Let NIL Be a One-Time Win

You don't have to be rich to start investing.

You just have to *start*.

Start with $50. Start with $100. Just start.

The earlier you invest, the less you'll have to hustle later.

Let your NIL check be the beginning—not the peak.

Let your money grow while *you* grow—on the field, in the classroom, and in life.

Because success isn't just getting paid once.

It's turning one opportunity into a lifetime of options.

Chapter 32: How to Start Investing – Your NIL Playbook for Building Wealth

Don't Just Get Paid. Build Something With It.

Let's keep it real—you just got your first NIL money. Whether it's $1,000 from a local brand or $10,000 from a bigger deal, you probably feel like celebrating. New sneakers? A trip with your crew? A flex on social media?

You've earned it.

But here's the truth: **if all you do is spend it, it won't last.**

This chapter is here to help you **make it last**—by investing. Because the real win isn't just getting paid today. It's building something that takes care of you *tomorrow*. That's what smart money moves do.

Step 1: What Is Investing?

Investing is what you do when you want your money to grow.

Instead of spending it or letting it sit in a basic checking account, you put your money into **things that can increase in value over time**—like stocks, bonds, or mutual funds.

Even if you start small and stay consistent, your money can grow on its own thanks to something called **compound interest**. That's when your money earns money—and then the money it earned also earns money. It builds like a snowball rolling downhill.

Step 2: Know What You're Saving For

Before you invest, ask yourself:

- **When will I need this money?**
- **Am I okay with some ups and downs in value?**
- **Am I building for the long run, or a short-term goal?**

If you're saving for something that's more than 5 years away—like your future, college, or life after sports—investing makes a lot of sense.

If it's something you'll need soon—like next semester's tuition or a car—keep that money in savings instead.

Step 3: Pick the Right Kind of Account

Not all investing accounts work the same way. Here's a quick overview of the ones that matter most for you:

Roth IRA

- You invest money you already paid taxes on
- It grows **tax-free**
- You can withdraw it in retirement without paying taxes
- You can only contribute if you **earned income**
- Max contribution: **$6,500/year (as of 2025)**

Why it's great: If you're a high school athlete earning NIL money, you're probably in a low tax bracket. That makes this a smart move—because the money grows *forever* without taxes.

Traditional IRA

- You might get a tax break now
- You pay taxes later when you take the money out
- Same contribution limit

This one is better for people who expect to make less money later in life—but it's still good to know about.

Taxable Brokerage Account

- No income or contribution limits
- You pay taxes on gains or dividends
- Full flexibility—you can use the money whenever

Why it's helpful: Great option if you already maxed out your Roth IRA, or if you need more flexibility.

Step 4: Let's Say You Got $100,000 From NIL

That's a big number. And it's exciting. But here's how to break it down like a pro:

First: Pay Your Taxes

NIL money isn't free from taxes. If no taxes are being taken out, **you need to save about 30%.**

$100,000 x 30% = $30,000 set aside just for taxes.

Don't touch it. Seriously.

Then: Fund a Roth IRA

If you're eligible, do it.

Max it out: $6,500 into a Roth IRA

Invest it in something like the S&P 500 index fund and let it grow—tax-free.

Next: Invest More in a Brokerage Account

You still have money left—don't waste it.

Put $30,000–$40,000 in a taxable brokerage account

Use ETFs or index funds. Stay consistent. Let it build.

Keep Some Cash On Hand

Stuff happens. NIL deals may slow down. Life doesn't.

Set aside $10,000–$15,000 in savings

This is your emergency fund. Don't skip this.

Reward Yourself (Within Limits)

You worked hard. Celebrate a little—but don't blow the whole bag.

Spend $5,000–$10,000 responsibly

Buy something meaningful. But be smart.

Your $100K Game Plan Recap

- $30,000 → Taxes
- $6,500 → Roth IRA
- $35,000 → Brokerage Account
- $15,000 → Emergency Savings
- $8,500 → Smart spending

That's how a future millionaire handles NIL money.

Step 5: No Big Check Yet? No Problem.

This plan works no matter what the number is.

Even if you only earned $1,000 or $2,000, the process stays the same:

- Save for taxes
- Invest what you can
- Build a cash cushion
- Spend the rest with purpose
- Repeat next time you get paid

Use automatic transfers. Keep it simple. Stay consistent.

Final Thoughts: One Check Shouldn't Be Your Peak

A lot of people get money and lose it just as fast.

Not you.

You're learning how to play the long game. That means taking some of that NIL money and putting it to work for *your future.*

Start investing now—even if it's just $50/month.

Because here's the truth:

- You don't need to be rich to start building wealth.
- You just need to start.
- And the earlier you do it, the easier it gets.

Let your NIL check be the first step in your legacy—not the end of your story.

You're not just an athlete.

You're a builder. A leader. A future millionaire in the making.

Let's go.

Chapter 33: Culture and Cash – How Your Background Shapes Your Money Mindset

Introduction: The Money You Carry Isn't Just in Your Wallet

When we talk about money, we're not just talking about income, taxes, credit scores, or investing. We're talking about the invisible weight that money carries in our lives — the emotions, stories, assumptions, fears, and expectations that come from how we were raised, where we come from, and the culture we belong to.

Whether you grew up in a single-parent household in the inner city, a two-parent military family in the suburbs, a tight-knit Tongan community, or an immigrant household where English was the second language — your money mindset is shaped by all of it.

For student-athletes, this matters even more. You're entering the NIL space with real money on the line, real decisions to make, and very few people who can relate to this new path you're walking. NIL is an opportunity to break cycles and build legacies — but to do that, you first have to understand what you're *carrying* with you into the game.

Section 1: Cultural Lenses – The Financial Mindsets We Inherit

Black Families

Historically, Black communities in the U.S. have faced systemic financial exclusion — redlining, job discrimination, denial of home loans, wage gaps. That trauma doesn't disappear — it gets passed down, sometimes silently. The result?

- Deep mistrust of financial institutions
- Emphasis on working harder, not necessarily smarter
- Tendency to equate spending with success ("looking like you made it")
- Loyalty to family, often at the expense of personal financial goals

In many Black families, you're taught to give back as soon as you get on. But if you don't learn how to build first, there won't be anything sustainable to give later.

White Families

In many white families — especially those with generational wealth or access to education — money is framed as a long-term planning tool. Parents might open IRAs for their kids, talk about 529 plans, use trust funds, or teach credit basics early. There may be less emotional charge around money and more structure. But this doesn't mean every white family is financially literate — many struggle silently, especially in blue-collar communities.

Latino Families

Family comes first. That's the thread across most Latino households. It's common for young earners to contribute to household bills, help with remittances, or support younger siblings. Conversations about money may be scarce, but expectations about responsibility are high. You may feel guilty for keeping your money — even if it's to invest in your future.

Asian-American Families

Many Asian cultures prioritize saving, frugality, and academic or career success. Financial decisions are often based on security and family image. There may be pressure to succeed in silence — to never let others see struggle. Investing may be viewed as risky, and debt may be avoided entirely. That mindset builds discipline but can also delay opportunities that come with calculated risks.

Tongan / Pacific Islander Families

Tongan and Pacific Islander cultures often stress communal values — sharing wealth with the broader family, honoring elders, and giving generously to church or community events. Success is seen as collective. That can be beautiful — but it also creates intense financial pressure on the first person in the family to "make it."

Middle Eastern Families

Money is often tied to status, family honor, and business acumen. There may be expectations to pursue professions like medicine, law, or engineering. Entrepreneurship is encouraged, but financial transparency is often limited to male figures. Sons may carry more financial responsibility; daughters may be shielded from money conversations altogether.

Section 2: Family Dynamics – How the Home You Grew Up in Affects Your Wallet

Let's break down a few common family structures and the financial beliefs they often create:

1. Single-Parent Households

- Often led by a hardworking parent doing it all.
- Kids may grow up fast, taking on financial responsibility early.
- Money may be scarce, but resilience is high.
- You may feel like it's your job to pay them back the moment you earn a dollar.

> Real Talk: *Giving back is noble. But building your financial foundation first is what* really *honors their sacrifice.*

2. Two-Parent Households (With Financial Tension)

- Money might be a source of conflict.
- You may have heard arguments about bills, spending, or debt.
- This can create financial *avoidance* — choosing not to talk or think about money.

> Reminder: *Avoiding money because it reminds you of conflict is like refusing to learn the playbook because you don't like the coach. You'll just lose.*

3. Multigenerational Households

- Grandparents, aunts, cousins — everyone's involved.
- You may have mixed messages about who's responsible for what.
- You may feel accountable to multiple adults — with different money

philosophies.

4. Financially Stable Households (But No Money Education)

- Everything looks fine from the outside.
- Bills are paid, vacations happen, cars are leased.
- But nobody's explaining *how* any of it works.

Lesson: Just because your parents seem stable doesn't mean they've taught you how to manage money. Ask.

Section 3: Emotional Habits Around Money

Ask Yourself:

- Do you feel **guilty** when you have more than your friends or family?
- Do you spend to **feel better** when life gets hard?
- Do you hide your money wins to avoid jealousy?
- Do you let others make money decisions for you because it's **easier**?

If any of these hit — you're not alone. But you have to start unlearning these habits if you want long-term success.

Section 4: Don't Let Uncle Jimmy Be Your Financial Advisor

Every culture has an "Uncle Jimmy." He means well. He's probably loud. He may have *opinions* on everything from crypto to buying land in "the metaverse."

But here's the deal:

Good intentions don't equal good information.

Don't take financial advice from:

- People who've never had to file NIL income taxes
- Family members who shame you for saving
- Coaches who only talk about "hustling" but not budgeting
- Friends who went viral once and now think they're financial gurus

Instead, seek:

- Certified financial planners (CFPs)
- CPAs with NIL experience
- Lawyers for contract review
- School compliance officers
- Your own research — not just TikTok "gurus"

Section 5: How to Talk to Your Family About Money

Start with curiosity, not confrontation:

"Hey Dad, how did you learn about money growing up?"

"Mom, what's one money lesson you want me to know?"

"If I wanted to start saving or investing, where do you think I should start?"

"I'm learning about NIL. Would you be open to talking with me about how we can handle it together?"

Keep it low-pressure:

Don't try to "fix" your family. Just open the door.

Section 6: 30+ Financial Conversation Starters for Families

Use these once a week or once a month. Mix and match by topic:

Money Memories

- What's the first big purchase you remember making?
- Did your parents talk to you about money growing up?
- What did money mean to you as a teenager?

Budgeting & Bills

- How do you decide what bills to pay first?
- What's the biggest expense in our house each month?
- Have you ever made a budget? Want to make one together?

Saving & Investing

- How did you start saving money when you were young?
- Have you ever invested? Why or why not?
- What's something you wish you'd saved for earlier?

Credit & Debt

- What's one thing I should know about credit cards?
- Have you ever had to fix your credit?
- Do you think debt is always bad?

Income & Work

- What was your first job, and how did you manage that money?
- Have you ever been underpaid?
- What's one lesson you learned from working hard?

Legacy & Goals

- What kind of life do you want for our family long-term?
- If you had extra money to invest or donate, what would you do with it?
- What's something you want me to do differently with money than you

did?

Section 7: Rules of Thumb to Carry With You

- **If you can't explain the investment, don't make it.**
- **It's okay to say "I don't know — let me ask a pro."**
- **Building wealth is quiet; flexing for likes is loud (and expensive).**
- **Every dollar you give away emotionally is a dollar you don't grow intentionally.**
- **You can still love your family and set financial boundaries.**
- **You don't have to play superhero with your NIL money.**
- **Never sign a contract you haven't had someone review.**
- **A good CPA is worth more than a fake "money mentor."**
- **The goal isn't just to make money — it's to keep it, grow it, and pass it down.**

Conclusion: Culture Is a Starting Point, Not a Limitation

The culture you come from is part of your story. But it doesn't have to limit your future. If your family didn't talk about money, **you get to be the one who starts the conversation.** If your parents struggled with debt, **you can be the one who builds credit wisely.** If nobody ever taught you about taxes, **you can be the first to hire a CPA and file it right.**

You are the bridge between what was and what can be.

Take what's beautiful from your culture — the community, the loyalty, the work ethic — and pair it with **knowledge, boundaries, and intentional growth.** That's how we change the game.

Chapter 34: Money Moves That Matter – How to Open Investment Accounts, Bank Smart, Build Credit, and Protect Your Scholarships

Start Early, Stay Ready

You're young. You're talented. You're earning money through NIL — or about to. Most people your age are *thinking* about their first job. You're thinking about taxes, contracts, scholarship eligibility, and how to make money moves that protect your future.

This chapter is your step-by-step guide to doing just that.

You'll learn:

- How to open your first **bank account**
- What's needed (and what's not)
- How to start **investing** (with a Roth IRA or traditional IRA)
- The **pros and cons** of getting your first credit card
- How to **use credit wisely**
- How NIL income might affect **college scholarships or aid**
- The right **questions to ask coaches and administrators**

You're not just playing the game. You're building your playbook.

Section 1: Opening Your First Bank Account

Before you invest, before you get a credit card, before you buy anything with NIL earnings — you need a checking and savings account.

Types of Bank Accounts

1. **Checking Account**

- Where you put money you'll spend soon (NIL payments, allowance, job income)
- Use for debit card transactions, paying bills, Venmo/CashApp links

1. **Savings Account**

- For money you don't plan to spend immediately
- Helps build discipline around saving for taxes, emergencies, or goals

> *Pro Tip: Choose a bank or credit union with low fees, good online access, and FDIC or NCUA insurance.*

What You Need to Open a Bank Account

Most banks will ask for:

- **Government-issued ID** (driver's license, passport, state ID)
- **Social Security Number** or ITIN
- **Address** (can be school, home, or guardian's if under 18)
- **Email + Phone Number**
- **Initial Deposit** (usually $25–$100, sometimes waived)

If you're under 18, you may need a **parent or guardian to co-sign**.

What You Don't Need

- A credit score (not for checking/savings)
- A job (you can deposit gift money, allowance, or NIL funds)
- A minimum balance (just avoid accounts with monthly fees!)

Questions to Ask the Bank

- Do you charge a monthly fee?
- Is there a minimum balance requirement?
- Do I get a debit card?
- Is there a mobile banking app?
- Are ATM withdrawals free?
- What happens if I overdraft?

> *Bonus Tip: Set up* ***text/email alerts*** *so you know every time money goes in or out. Protect your bag.*

Section 2: Opening a Roth IRA or Traditional IRA – Yes, You Can Start Investing NOW

What Is an IRA?

IRA = Individual Retirement Account

There are two main types:

1. **Roth IRA**

- You invest after-tax money now
- Grows tax-free
- You don't pay taxes when you withdraw in retirement

1. **Traditional IRA**

- You invest pre-tax money (or write it off at tax time)
- You pay taxes when you take it out later

> *For most young athletes with NIL income, a* ***Roth IRA is the move.*** *You're likely in a low tax bracket now, so paying taxes upfront makes sense.*

Who Can Open One?

If you have earned income (NIL counts as 1099 self-employment income), **you can contribute up to $7,000 per year** (as of 2025).

You *must* open the account with money you earned — not from gifts or allowances.

Where to Open One

- Fidelity
- Vanguard
- Charles Schwab
- E*TRADE
- Betterment
- Acorns
- Robinhood (not ideal for long-term retirement but okay for starters)

Look for:

- No minimums
- No account fees
- Free trading for ETFs or index funds

What You'll Need to Open One

- Name + Address
- Social Security Number
- Bank account info for funding
- Photo ID
- Employment income (NIL deals count — keep documentation)

> *Tip: Keep contracts and 1099 forms from your NIL deals. They prove your earned income.*

What to Invest In

- **Target Date Funds** (set it and forget it based on your age)
- **Index Funds** (like S&P 500)
- **ETFs** (diversified, low-cost)

Start small. Consistency beats perfection.

Section 3: Your First Credit Card – Build Credit Without Breaking the Bank

Why You Should Get One (Eventually)

Credit cards aren't evil — *misused* credit cards are. Used wisely, a beginner card helps you:

- Build your **credit score**
- Get better **loan rates** in the future
- Qualify for **apartment leases, phones, or cars**
- Teach you how to handle debt responsibly

How to Qualify

- Be at least 18
- Have some income (NIL counts!)
- Possibly get a **co-signer** or open a **student credit card**

Types of Beginner Cards

1. **Student Credit Card** – Designed for college students
2. **Secured Credit Card** – Requires a cash deposit as collateral
3. **Retail or Store Card** – Easier to qualify but often high interest
4. **Credit Builder Card** – Limited spending, designed to help you start

Credit Card Terms to Understand

Term What It Means

APR

Interest rate charged if you don't pay in full

Credit Limit

The max you can spend on the card

Minimum Payment

The smallest amount due each month

Grace Period

Time between the bill and interest starting

Pros of Having a Card

- Builds credit history
- Creates financial independence
- Teaches discipline and responsibility

- May offer rewards or cashback

Cons (If Misused)

- High-interest debt adds up fast
- Can hurt your credit if you miss payments
- Easy to overspend
- Missed payments stay on your report for 7 **years**

Rules of the Game

- Only spend what you can pay in FULL each month
- Use **less than 30%** of your credit limit (preferably under 10%)
- Set **auto-pay** for the full balance
- Never use it for "fun" purchases unless you have the cash already

> *Example: If your credit limit is $500, never carry a balance over $150.*

Section 4: Will NIL Deals Affect Your College Scholarships or Financial Aid?

Here's What You Need to Know

NIL is considered earned income. That means:

- It may impact **need-based aid** (like Pell Grants or state grants)
- It generally **won't impact athletic scholarships**, but you must follow school compliance rules
- You'll need to **report NIL earnings on the FAFSA**

Who Should You Talk To?

- **Financial Aid Office** – To ask how your NIL money affects need-based aid
- **Compliance Officer** – To stay NCAA-eligible and avoid violations
- **College Coach** – They may know the policies or support resources
- **CPA or Tax Preparer** – To report NIL income properly

Questions to Ask Your School

- Does the school reduce scholarship awards based on outside income?
- Will my NIL money affect housing stipends or meal plans?
- Can I receive NIL income and still keep my current aid?
- Is there someone on campus who can help me file taxes?
- Do I need to report all NIL deals to the school or NCAA?

Section 5: Protect Your Paper – Don't Lose What You Earned

Keep Your Documents

- All NIL contracts
- 1099 tax forms
- Proof of expenses
- Banking records
- Investment account confirmations

Red Flags to Avoid

- Advisors or agents asking for cash upfront
- Contracts with no end date or exit clause
- Schools telling you "not to worry about it" (ask anyway!)
- Friends wanting to "help" but not offering real credentials

Build a 3-Account System

1. **Spending Account** - Everyday expenses
2. **Savings Account** - Emergency fund + taxes
3. **Investing Account** - Long-term growth (Roth IRA)

This structure keeps you organized and disciplined.

Conclusion: Every Account You Open is a Step Toward Independence

Opening a bank account, getting a credit card, starting an investment plan — these aren't just adulting chores. They're game changers. Every smart move you make now puts you ahead later. And the sooner you learn, the better you'll play the financial game for life.

Your NIL money is powerful. But *how you manage it*? That's where the real power is.

So start now. Ask questions. Set your accounts up. Build habits. And make sure that when you earn more — you're ready for more.

Chapter 35: CONCLUSION Be a Pro Before You Go Pro

You've made it to the end of this book—but your NIL journey is just getting started.

Whether you're a freshman preparing for your first varsity tryout or a senior getting ready for Signing Day, one thing is clear: **you don't have to wait to be a professional to think like one.**

In fact, in today's world of NIL, social media, branding, and opportunity, the most successful athletes—the ones who rise, last, and lead—aren't just the strongest or the fastest.

They're the ones who are **mentally prepared**, **financially educated**, and **personally grounded** before the spotlight ever finds them.

Why Starting Early Changes Everything

When you start thinking about your money, your brand, and your mindset in high school, you give yourself something most athletes never have: **time.**

Time to make mistakes while the stakes are low.

Time to build strong habits that last.

Time to learn how to handle success *before* it overwhelms you.

Too many athletes wait until they're already on a college roster—or worse, already in a deal—to start asking basic questions:

> *"What's a 1099?"*

"Can I get in trouble for this post?"
"How do taxes work?"
"Who owns my content?"
"Can I really say no to this contract?"

By then, the pressure's real. The mistakes cost more. And the brand damage can be permanent.

But not for you.

By reading this book, doing the work, and having the conversations early and often, you're choosing to **lead yourself first**—before anyone else leads you in the wrong direction.

Protecting Your Mind, Money, and Name

There's a lot of talk in the NIL world about "building your brand" and "securing the bag."

But before the brand and the bag, you have to protect three things that will always matter more:

Your Mind

- Stay grounded. Don't let hype change who you are.
- Take breaks from social media when it gets overwhelming.
- Surround yourself with people who care more about *you* than what you can do for them.
- Find mentors who challenge you, not just cheer for you.

Your Money

- Keep your receipts.
- Track your income.
- Save more than you spend.
- Ask questions before signing anything.

- Think long-term. Always.

Money can open doors—or cause drama. How you handle it early says everything about the future you're building.

Your Name

- Your name is on every contract you sign.
- Your name is on every post you publish.
- Your name is what brands invest in—and what fans remember.

Protect it like your jersey number. Don't lend it out for cheap clicks or fast cash.

Because long after the lights go out, **your name is what people will still talk about.**

Leaving a Legacy On and Off the Field

The truth is, not everyone will go pro in sports.

But **every athlete can go pro in life.**

You can build a business.

You can give back to your community.

You can teach others how to avoid the mistakes you were smart enough to dodge.

You can walk into any room with confidence, because you know what you're worth—and you know how to protect it.

That's what this is really about.

Not just being the face of a brand—but being the kind of person **people are proud to follow.**

Not just making NIL money—but making **decisions that change your family's future.**

Not just scoring points—but **setting an example** your younger teammates, siblings, and followers can look up to.

That's how you build a legacy.

And legacy > clout. Every single time.

Final Message

You don't need to be famous to be focused.

You don't need to have followers to be financially smart.

You don't need to wait for college to act like a professional.

Be a pro before you go pro.

In your mindset.

In your money habits.

In your NIL decisions.

In the way you represent your name, your family, and your future.

Because the real win isn't just making money—it's **making it matter.**

And now, you're ready to do just that.

About the Author

Pat Brown, MBA is a former Division I football captain turned nationally recognized financial educator and advocate. After playing linebacker for the University of Kansas, where he helped lead his team to a top 10 national ranking and earned the prestigious Iron Hawk Award, Pat went on to play professionally in the Canadian Football League. But it was off the field where he found his true calling — helping others build financial security and long-term wealth.

As a financial advisor with over two decades of experience, Pat has counseled everyone from retirees and professionals to student-athletes and families just starting their journey. His passion for financial literacy was born from personal experience. As a student-athlete himself, he realized how little financial education was offered to young athletes — especially those from underserved communities — and how dangerous that gap could be once money started coming in.

That realization became a mission.

Pat is the founder of multiple platforms dedicated to empowering others through financial education, including **Financial Literacy for NIL**, **Financial Literacy for Student-Athletes**, **Financial Literacy for The Culture**, and **Financial Literacy for Parents of Student-Athletes**, among others. His work spans speaking engagements, community outreach, curriculum design, and authoring a full series of books that bridge the gap between money and mindset.

He speaks regularly at high schools, colleges, churches, hospitals, and leadership panels, and serves on several community boards, including Lawrence Memorial Hospital and the KU K-Club. Pat is also a devoted husband and father to two college-aged daughters, continuing a legacy of service, leadership, and family support — the same values that guide his work today.

This book is more than just a guide — it's personal. Pat wrote it to give student-athletes and their families a game plan to not only survive, but thrive in the NIL era and beyond.

Learn more at: www.financialliteracyfornil.com

100 Questions High School Student-Athletes Can Ask About NIL and Financial Literacy

For College Coaches, School Administrators, Compliance Officers, CPAs, Financial Advisors, NIL Agents, and Business Managers

Questions to Ask Yourself

1. What do I know about NIL right now?
2. Am I ready to manage money if I start earning it?
3. What are my long-term goals beyond sports?
4. What does success look like for me off the field?
5. Do I know how to budget or save?
6. How do I define my personal brand?
7. Who do I trust to help me make financial decisions?
8. What kind of content do I post, and does it help or hurt my brand?
9. Do I have a plan for taxes?
10. Do I know what kind of advisor or mentor I need?

Questions to Ask Parents/Guardians

1. How do you manage money in our household?
2. Have you ever worked with a financial advisor or CPA?
3. What do you wish someone told you about money when you were my age?

4. How should I save for taxes if I start making NIL money?
5. Can we go over a basic budget together?

Questions to Ask High School Coaches

1. Does our school offer NIL education or training?
2. Are we allowed to sign NIL deals right now?
3. What are the school or state rules for high school NIL?
4. Who do I talk to if a brand reaches out to me?
5. What risks should I know about when dealing with NIL?

Questions to Ask High School Counselors/Administrators

1. Are there financial literacy courses I can take?
2. What GPA and test scores do I need to remain eligible for scholarships?
3. Will earning NIL money affect my college aid or FAFSA?
4. Can you help me understand the difference between financial aid and scholarships?
5. How do I track NCAA-eligible courses on my transcript?

Questions to Ask College Coaches

1. What is your school's NIL policy?
2. Do you help athletes find or manage NIL opportunities?
3. Are there NIL collectives affiliated with your program?
4. What NIL support or education do you provide players?
5. If I make money through NIL, does that impact my scholarship?
6. Can NIL income affect my playing time or standing with the team?
7. Do you allow athletes to bring their own agents or advisors?
8. How do you protect athletes from bad NIL deals?
9. Have athletes at your school had any problems with NIL?
10. How do you help incoming freshmen navigate NIL?

Questions to Ask College Compliance/Administration

1. How do I report NIL deals at your school?
2. Are there NIL restrictions specific to your state?
3. Do you have an NIL disclosure or tracking portal?
4. Can athletes work with agents while maintaining eligibility?
5. How does NIL income affect housing, meal stipends, or cost of attendance?
6. Will I need to set up an LLC or business entity?
7. Who reviews NIL contracts before I sign them?
8. Can I get help filing taxes on NIL income?
9. Do you offer any financial literacy programs for athletes?
10. What happens if I accidentally violate NIL policy?

Questions to Ask CPAs or Tax Professionals

1. How do I report NIL income on my taxes?
2. What's the difference between a W-2 and a 1099?
3. Do I need to make quarterly estimated tax payments?
4. What deductions can I claim as a student-athlete?
5. Can my parents still claim me as a dependent if I earn NIL income?
6. Should I open a separate bank account for NIL income?
7. How do I track NIL expenses for write-offs?
8. What's the best way to prepare for an audit?
9. Do you recommend I hire a bookkeeper?
10. When should I hire a CPA instead of doing taxes myself?

Questions to Ask Financial Advisors

1. What's the difference between a fiduciary and a financial advisor?
2. Can you help me budget NIL income?
3. How much should I save vs. spend?
4. Can you help me open a Roth IRA or investment account?

5. What are smart first investments for young athletes?
6. How can I build credit responsibly while in college?
7. How do I set financial goals?
8. Should I pay off debt before investing?
9. How do I know if an advisor is legit?
10. Do you offer ongoing coaching or one-time planning?

Questions to Ask NIL Agents or Marketing Reps

1. Are you registered or licensed to work with athletes?
2. What percentage do you charge for managing deals?
3. Will you help me grow my brand or just sign deals?
4. Do I still own my content and likeness?
5. How do you find brand opportunities for your clients?
6. Do you work with any athletes I'd know?
7. Can I see sample contracts before signing with you?
8. How do you handle exclusivity?
9. Do you offer legal review of contracts?
10. What happens if I want to end the relationship?

Questions to Ask Business Managers or Brand Advisors

1. Can you help me manage both personal and business expenses?
2. Do you offer monthly or quarterly reporting?
3. How do you protect my money and privacy?
4. Can you coordinate with my CPA and advisor?
5. Do you charge hourly, monthly, or a percentage?
6. What services do you include beyond basic accounting?
7. How do I know my NIL brand is protected legally?
8. Can you help me license my name or logo?
9. How do I prevent others from using my brand without permission?
10. Can you help me structure a business or nonprofit?

General NIL and Financial Literacy Questions

1. What's the difference between being an employee vs. independent contractor?
2. Do I need an LLC to do NIL deals?
3. What are red flags in NIL contracts?
4. How can I build my brand without getting in trouble?
5. What is self-employment tax and how much should I save?
6. What happens if I break an NIL contract?
7. Can NIL income disqualify me from financial aid?
8. How do I manage peer pressure around money?
9. Can I make NIL money in high school and still stay eligible?
10. What should I post on social media to attract brands?
11. Can I give money to my family without tax issues?
12. What happens if I earn NIL money in multiple states?
13. What financial tools or apps should I use to track NIL income?
14. Who should be part of my NIL team?
15. What's the one money habit I should start today?

Important Dates

TAX-RELATED DATES (Federal and State)

- January 1: Begin organizing prior year's financial records, including NIL income, receipts, and contracts
- January 15: Due date for 4th Quarter estimated tax payment from previous year (for NIL or self-employment income)
- January 31: Deadline for businesses and brands to send 1099-NEC forms and W-2s to recipients
- February 1: Begin gathering bank statements, expense summaries, and mileage logs for tax preparation
- April 1: Deadline to request tuition payment records (Form 1098-T) from your college for potential tax credits
- April 15: Federal tax filing deadline (unless extended)
- April 15: Deadline to contribute to a Roth IRA or Traditional IRA for the prior tax year
- April 15: 1st Quarter estimated tax payment due for current year
- June 15: 2nd Quarter estimated tax payment due
- September 15: 3rd Quarter estimated tax payment due
- October 15: Extended tax return deadline (only if extension was filed by April 15)

RETIREMENT & INVESTMENT CONTRIBUTIONS (2025 figures)

- January 1 – December 31: Eligible window to contribute to employer-sponsored retirement plans like 401(k) or 403(b) (limit: $23,000 under age 50)
- January 1 – April 15 (following year): Eligible window to contribute to a Roth IRA or Traditional IRA for the previous year (limit: $7,000 under age 50)
- December 31: Final date to make charitable contributions that may count as deductions for the current year
- Ongoing: Monitor NIL earnings for Roth IRA eligibility (must have documented earned income)
- Ongoing: Maintain records of any brokerage investment activity for capital gains tax reporting

NCAA / NAIA / NJCAA COMPLIANCE & ELIGIBILITY

- Freshman Year (High School): Begin tracking NCAA-required courses and GPA minimums
- Sophomore Year: Monitor NCAA eligibility progress and consider creating an athletic résumé
- Start of Junior Year: Register with NCAA Eligibility Center (eligibilitycenter.org)
- Junior Year Spring: Schedule campus visits; verify school NIL policies and state laws
- Fall of Senior Year: Submit official transcripts and standardized test scores to NCAA/NAIA using code 9999
- August 1: New NCAA policies typically take effect each academic year
- Preseason/Summer: Meet with compliance office to update NIL disclosures, academic status, and endorsement history
- Every Semester: Maintain minimum GPA and full-time enrollment for eligibility

- Every Time You Sign an NIL Deal: Notify your school's compliance officer (use your school's portal if applicable)

COLLEGE & ATHLETIC ADMISSIONS TIMELINE

- August–September (Senior Year): Narrow down target colleges and athletic programs
- September 1: NCAA allows contact between D1 coaches and senior athletes (sport-dependent)
- October 1: FAFSA opens for the next academic year
- October 15 – November 1: Early decision and early action college application deadlines begin
- November 8–15: National Signing Day window for many NCAA sports (fall signing period)
- December 1–15: Most schools' early action/early decision notifications released
- January 1–15: Regular decision deadlines for many universities
- March 1: Priority FAFSA deadline for many colleges (state-specific deadlines may be earlier)
- April 1–15: Admission notifications and financial aid award letters released
- May 1: National College Decision Day—deadline to commit and submit enrollment deposit
- May 15 – July 1: Final opportunity to submit high school transcripts to colleges

HIGH SCHOOL TESTING DATES (SAT, ACT, AP Exams, State Testing)

SAT 2025

- March 8, 2025 (Register by Feb 7)
- May 3, 2025 (Register by April 4)
- June 7, 2025 (Register by May 2)

ACT 2025

- April 12, 2025 (Register by March 7)
- June 14, 2025 (Register by May 9)
- July 12, 2025 (Register by June 6)

AP Exams (Advanced Placement)

- First two weeks of May: College Board AP exams for college credit
- (Common for student-athletes at academically rigorous high schools)

State Graduation Exams

- Varies by state: Typically administered between March and June
- (Check with your school counselor for state-specific graduation requirements)

YEARLY CONVERSATIONS TO HAVE EARLY & OFTEN

Because Your Future Deserves More Than One Talk

When it comes to NIL, money, and life after high school, there's one truth that every student-athlete needs to hear:

You can't afford to "figure it out later."

Big decisions don't come with warm-up drills. When the offer is in front of you, the contract is in your inbox, or the season is flying by—you need to be ready.

And readiness doesn't come from guessing. It comes from **having the right conversations with the right people at the right time—every year**.

This chapter is your guide to those conversations.

It's not about one dramatic sit-down or a "money talk" after you sign a deal. It's about **building a culture of communication**—with your parents, coaches, mentors, and professionals—so you're never caught off guard.

👨‍👩‍👧‍👦 WITH PARENTS/GUARDIANS: Talk Early. Talk Often.

Your family—whether that's your parents, grandparents, or guardians—will be your first NIL support system. Even if you're the one playing, they're likely the ones helping you manage money, fill out forms, talk to advisors, and stay grounded.

So you need to keep them in the loop, **every year**, not just when something big happens.

✐ *Expectations for Money Management*

As soon as money is on the table—or even the idea of it—make sure you and your family are on the same page.

Questions to revisit every year:

- "If I earn NIL money, who will help manage it?"
- "Where will the money go—savings, spending, investing, helping the family?"
- "How much should I set aside for taxes?"
- "Do we need to open new bank accounts or create a budget?"
- "What do we do if the money starts changing how people treat us?"

Why this matters:

Money can bring stress, especially when family dynamics are involved. Setting expectations early helps prevent conflict later. It also keeps you focused on using money **as a tool—not a distraction.**

✐ *College Savings and Financial Aid Strategy*

Even if you're dreaming of a full-ride scholarship, don't stop planning.

NIL money could help with:

- SAT/ACT prep or tutoring
- Application fees
- Campus visits
- Dorm supplies and textbooks
- Tuition gaps if your scholarship doesn't cover everything

But here's the twist: **NIL income can also impact your eligibility for financial aid.** If your family fills out the FAFSA, NIL money might need to be reported.

Talk about:

- "Are we saving for college—and how much do we have?"
- "What scholarships or aid are we hoping for?"
- "If I earn money, will that reduce the aid I'm eligible for?"
- "Should we meet with a financial aid officer or college counselor?"

✓ *What to Do If a Deal Is Offered*

You don't want to be scrambling when an offer comes in. Have this talk before it happens, so you have a plan in place.

Discuss:

- "What's our first step if a company wants to work with me?"
- "Who will review the contract?"
- "How will we respond to DMs, emails, or phone calls?"
- "Do we say yes to everything—or only to certain kinds of brands?"
- "Will I need to turn down opportunities to stay focused on school or sports?"

Having this framework in place allows you to act quickly—but wisely.

Pro tip: Role-play the moment. Have someone send you a fake NIL offer. Practice reviewing it together. That way, you're ready when it's real.

WITH COACHES AND ATHLETIC DIRECTORS: Build Trust Through Transparency

Your coach and AD are more than game-day guides. They're gatekeepers to your eligibility, reputation, and college exposure. And when it comes to NIL, they're also navigating new territory right alongside you.

Make it a habit to check in with them each year—not just about your stats, but about your **future off the field**.

✅ *NIL Rules, School Policies, and Athlete Support*

Every school—and every state—has its own NIL rules. Your coach or athletic director should know where you stand.

Ask:

- "Are high school NIL deals allowed in our state?"
- "What are our school's policies around NIL?"
- "Can I use our team uniform or school logo in my content?"
- "Are there any deals I'm not allowed to accept?"
- "Do you know of any athletes who've done NIL before—what worked or didn't?"

Even if the rules haven't changed since last year, **reconfirm every season**. Laws evolve. Schools update their policies. Don't assume.

✅ *How to Balance Performance and Outside Opportunities*

The biggest concern most coaches have about NIL? **That it will become a distraction.** They want to know you're still locked in on your craft, your teammates, and your role.

Be proactive and ask:

- "How can I make sure NIL doesn't interfere with our season?"
- "Is there a good time during the year to pursue deals—or times I should avoid?"
- "Would it help if I shared a list of any deals I'm considering?"

If you show respect and transparency, your coach is more likely to support your efforts—and even connect you with helpful contacts.

🧑‍🏫💼 WITH MENTORS AND PROFESSIONALS: Build Your Future Team, Not Just Your Deal Team

Every athlete needs a circle of wisdom—people who understand money, business, and life, even if they've never played your sport.

This might include:

- A teacher or principal you trust
- A financial advisor or CPA
- A local business owner or entrepreneur
- A college athlete who's already in the NIL space

✅ *When to Bring in Legal/Financial Help*

Here's the rule: **If you don't fully understand what you're signing, don't sign.**

NIL contracts are legally binding, and taxes don't care if you "didn't know better."

Ask a mentor:

- "When should I hire help—and what kind of help do I need?"
- "Do you know any trustworthy advisors, agents, or attorneys I can talk to?"
- "What's the difference between someone who's 'for me' and someone who's just 'using me'?"

If you're under 18, your parent or guardian will likely need to sign contracts on your behalf—but **you should still understand what you're agreeing to**.

✅ *How to Vet Contracts and Partnerships*

Most bad NIL deals don't look bad at first. That's why you need help reading between the lines.

Ask your mentor to help you:

- Read sample NIL contracts
- Understand terms like exclusivity, deliverables, royalties, usage rights, and termination
- Recognize pressure tactics or vague promises
- Spot deals that could hurt your eligibility or image

Also—don't forget your value. A mentor can help you assess whether the deal is worth your time, effort, and alignment with your goals.

✅ *Building a Long-Term Mindset—Not Just Short-Term Cash*

This is one of the most important conversations you can have with any mentor or advisor:

"How do I use NIL to build my future—not just my bank account?"

Short-term money is exciting. Long-term stability is powerful.

Talk about:

- Saving vs. spending
- Brand building beyond high school
- Using NIL to grow into entrepreneurship, real estate, or investment
- Giving back to your community or creating impact

Let someone older than you help you **zoom out**. Ask them what they wish they'd known at your age.

Conversation Timeline: When to Have These Talks

Topic/ Who to Talk To/ When to Have the Conversation

Money management & budgeting
Parent/Guardian
Start of each semester/year
NIL eligibility & school policy
Coach/AD
Preseason or at team meetings
Contract/legal help
Mentor or advisor
Before signing any agreement
Tax readiness
Parent/CPA/Advisor
Beginning of the year & before tax season
College NIL communication
College coach or compliance officer
After commitment or signing day
Financial aid & scholarships
Counselor/Parent
When applying for college
Brand review
Mentor or trusted adult
Mid-year check-in
Set reminders. Revisit. Don't assume a one-time talk covers it all.

📋 Your Annual NIL Conversation Checklist

✅ I've talked with my family about money, saving, spending, and tax expectations

✅ I've reviewed my school's NIL policy with my coach or athletic director

✅ I've asked my future college about their NIL rules and support

✅ I've built a list of mentors or professionals I can ask for help

✅ I've reviewed sample NIL contracts with someone I trust

✅ I've had at least one conversation about long-term goals and financial planning

✅ I've updated my budget or savings plan based on new NIL earnings

✅ I've asked for help before agreeing to anything I didn't fully understand

✅ I've made it a habit to ask questions—even when it's uncomfortable

🔚 Final Thoughts: Conversations Build Confidence

When you take the lead in these yearly conversations, you stop being just a "prospect"—and start becoming a professional.

You're not just learning how to navigate NIL.

You're learning how to communicate. To advocate. To lead.

And that's what real success is built on.

So don't wait for emergencies to start talking.

Don't wait for a check to start asking.

And don't let fear or pride keep you from reaching out.

Conversations open doors. And the earlier and more often you have them, the more prepared—and powerful—you'll be.

Year-by-Year NIL Game Plan Worksheet

Freshman Year: Learn Before You Earn

- Understand what NIL means and how it affects you
- Set academic, athletic, and financial goals
- Clean up and curate your social media presence
- Open a savings account and start a simple budget
- Ask parents/guardians about college savings
- Track school and state rules regarding NIL eligibility
- Identify 1–2 mentors you can turn to for advice

Sophomore Year: Build Your Foundation

- Create a content calendar (sports, school, personality)
- Start engaging with local community and brands
- Learn about taxes, contracts, and saving strategies
- Practice a mock NIL budget with a sample $1,000 deal
- Draft a one-page bio or media kit
- Schedule yearly check-ins with family, coach, mentor

Junior Year: Position for Opportunity

- Begin tracking your performance + engagement metrics
- Talk to your school and coach about NIL policies
- Meet with a financial advisor or CPA for tax basics
- Identify potential local NIL partners and sponsors
- Create folders for receipts, agreements, and documents

- Update your brand visuals, voice, and content style
- Begin reaching out to college programs about NIL readiness

Senior Year: Finalize Your Readiness

- Communicate with your future college about NIL compliance
- Review a sample contract with an adult or legal advisor
- Reassess your goals: academic, financial, personal
- Complete a year-end social media audit
- Create a post-graduation money plan
- Finalize your NIL team: mentor, financial, legal, brand
- Write your final NIL resume + story

Social Media Brand Audit Checklist

Your social media tells the world who you are. Make sure it tells the right story.

Bio:

- Includes name, sport, school, grad year
- Reflects personality or values
- Includes a contact link (Beacons, Linktree, etc.)

Posts:

- Last 10 posts reflect consistency and purpose
- Content includes a balance of sports, academics, and personal values
- No posts that could harm your brand or eligibility
- Captions are clean, intentional, and positive
- Hashtags are appropriate and useful

Engagement:

- You regularly reply to comments or DMs professionally
- You follow relevant brands, athletes, and college programs
- You avoid arguments, drama, or trolling

Visuals:

- Profile and cover photos are high-quality and current
- Highlight stories are organized and relevant (Games, School, Family, etc.)
- You showcase your personality (humor, hobbies, passions)

Growth Plan:

- You post regularly (1–3 times per week)
- You tell stories—not just drop stats
- You show gratitude to teammates, coaches, sponsors, and fans
- You use social media to lead—not just follow

Sample NIL Term Sheet (Expanded & Explained)

This is a fictional example created for educational purposes to show what a typical high school or early-college level NIL agreement might look like.

Athlete Name:

Jalen Carter
Senior, Lincoln High School
Basketball | Class of 2025

Brand:

Local Grille & Smoothie Bar
A neighborhood restaurant and smoothie bar known for sponsoring local athletes and promoting healthy lifestyle choices in the community.

Deal Duration:

April 15 – June 30, 2025
This agreement is in effect for approximately 2.5 months. That means:

- All content must be created and posted during this window.
- The athlete may not promote any competing brands during this time

(see exclusivity).
- Once the term ends, no additional obligations apply unless the deal is renewed or extended.

Deliverables (What Jalen is expected to do):

1. **Two Instagram posts**

- Must tag the business's official handle: @localsmoothie
- Must include 1 in uniform or branded athletic apparel and 1 in casual attire
- Caption must mention the business by name and include one of the approved hashtags: #FuelWithSmoothie, #LocalGrilleAthlete

1. **One TikTok video**

- 30–60 seconds in length
- Must include an authentic review of Jalen's favorite smoothie
- Must tag the business account and include a brand-provided promotional code for followers (e.g., "JALEN10" for a 10% discount)

1. **One in-person appearance**

- 1-hour community meet-and-greet at Local Grille's location on **Saturday, May 15th, 2025**
- Jalen must wear clean team-approved apparel and participate in 1 group photo and 1 short video clip (posted by the business)

*These deliverables clearly outline **how many**, **what kind**, and **when** Jalen must complete the marketing activities. All parties should agree on these specifics in advance.*

Compensation (What Jalen receives in return):

- **$500** total, paid **via PayPal** within 7 days of completing the final deliverable (after the appearance on May 15)
- **Free smoothie** of his choice on any visit during the deal period (limit: 1 per day)

This shows that the deal is partly paid in ***cash*** *and partly in* ***non-cash (in-kind) compensation.*** *All compensation should be clearly defined—including payment method and timeline.*

Exclusivity Clause (Limits on working with other brands):

- Jalen **may not promote** any other **food or beverage brand** (including national chains, other local restaurants, or energy drink companies) for the duration of the agreement, **April 15 – June 30**.
- This applies to **social media content, appearances, and sponsorships.**

This protects the brand from "split loyalty" or competitor promotion. It's a ***common clause*** *in NIL contracts—but make sure it doesn't interfere with bigger opportunities.*

Usage Rights (Who owns the content):

- Local Grille may **repost** or **share** Jalen's content on:
- Their social media accounts (Instagram, Facebook, TikTok)
- Their website or promotional emails
- The brand **may not** use the content for:
- Paid advertising
- Print materials or billboards
- Television or other media without additional permission
- Jalen retains **ownership of all original content** and may repost it on

his own platforms.

This clause ensures that the business can use the content—but only within agreed channels. ***Athletes should always understand where and how their image may appear.***

Termination Clause (How to end the agreement early):

- Either Jalen or Local Grille may cancel the agreement with 7 **days' written notice.**
- If either party ends the deal early:
- The athlete will be compensated **only for work completed** at the time of termination.
- Any unfinished deliverables will be removed from the contract.

Termination clauses protect ***both parties.*** *They give flexibility if something changes or if the relationship isn't working out.*

Additional Notes and Conditions:

- **Content must align with school district and athletic association NIL policies.**
- If Jalen's state or school changes its NIL stance, or if he violates school code, this deal may be reviewed or adjusted.
- **Deliverable proof:**
- Jalen must submit screenshots or links **within 24 hours** of posting content. This can be via email or shared folder.
- **Conduct clause:**
- If the athlete is suspended from school or faces major disciplinary action, the brand reserves the right to suspend or cancel the agreement.

🔍 Key Takeaways from This Sample Deal

✅ *Clear Expectations*

Jalen knows exactly **what he needs to do**, how often, and where (Instagram, TikTok, appearance).

✅ *Payment Plan*

The business outlines **how much he'll be paid**, **when he'll be paid**, and **how the payment will be delivered**—along with a bonus (free smoothies).

✅ *Fair Exclusivity*

He can't promote competing brands during the contract window—but the clause is limited in time and scope (which is reasonable).

✅ *Athlete Protection*

He keeps **ownership of his content**, and there's a clear **termination policy** in case the deal needs to end early.

✅ *Compliance and Conduct Covered*

The deal respects **school and state policies**, which protects Jalen's eligibility and integrity.

⚠□ What to Always Watch for in a Term Sheet or NIL Deal:

- **Are the deliverables too vague or too demanding?**
- **Is the pay clear—and is it fair?**
- **Are there any surprises in the exclusivity clause?**
- **Do you understand what the brand can do with your content?**

- **Can you get out of the deal if needed—and how?**
- **Does this align with your values, your goals, and your public image?**

If **anything is unclear, missing, or feels off—stop and ask.** Bring in a parent, coach, or advisor. It's better to wait and review than to rush and regret.

✍□ Reflection Questions for the Reader:

1. If you were offered a deal like this, what questions would you ask before signing?
2. Would you feel comfortable with the exclusivity clause?
3. Would this deal interfere with school, sports, or other priorities?
4. How would you keep records of your content and payments?
5. Is this a brand you would want to be associated with long-term?

Glossary of Financial + NIL Terms Every Athlete Should Know

Your go-to guide for understanding the business behind your brand. This glossary is more than just definitions—it's a playbook to help you make smart decisions, avoid mistakes, and take ownership of your future. Whether you're reviewing a contract, meeting with a mentor, or just learning the game, this list gives you the tools to speak the language of NIL with confidence.

A–C

1099 Form

A tax form used to report non-employee income, typically from freelance work or contract jobs. As a student-athlete, if you earn $600 or more from a brand or NIL deal, you'll likely receive a 1099 form from that company at the end of the year.

Accountability

Being responsible for your actions, money, reputation, and commitments. In NIL, this means doing what you say you'll do—whether that's posting content, showing up to an appearance, or responding professionally to brands.

Accrued Interest

The interest that accumulates on a loan, credit card, or investment over time but hasn't been paid or received yet.

Agent

A person who helps negotiate deals and manage brand partnerships. Only work with agents who are registered and transparent about their fees.

Amateurism

Your status as a non-professional athlete, which allows you to compete in high school and college sports. NIL lets you earn money without giving up your amateur status—as long as you follow the rules.

Annual Fee

A yearly fee charged by some credit card companies just to use the card.

APR (Annual Percentage Rate)

The yearly cost of borrowing money, shown as a percentage. Applies to loans and credit cards.

Assets

Things of value that you own—this includes your name, image, likeness, social media audience, and future earnings.

Audit

A review of your financial records, usually by the IRS. Keep detailed NIL income and expense records to stay audit-ready.

Auto-Pay

A feature that pays your bills automatically from your bank account or credit card to avoid late fees.

Bank Statement

A summary of all activity in your bank account over a specific time period.

Brand

Your reputation and the impression people have when they hear your name or see your content.

Budget

A written plan that helps you manage money—what's coming in (income) and what's going out (spending, saving, taxes).

Capital Gains

The profit from selling an investment for more than you paid.

Cash Flow

The total amount of money moving in and out of your accounts.

Chargeback

A transaction reversal usually due to a dispute or fraud.

Compound Interest

Interest calculated on both the initial principal and accumulated interest.

CPA (Certified Public Accountant)

A licensed financial expert who helps with taxes, income tracking, deductions, and reporting.

Credit Limit

The maximum amount you can spend using your credit card.

Credit Report

A summary of your credit history including balances, payment history, and credit inquiries.

Credit Score

A three-digit number representing your creditworthiness, based on credit history.

Contract

A legal agreement that outlines the expectations, payment, timelines, and rules between you and a brand or representative.

D–H

Debt

Money that is owed or due to another party.

Default

Failure to pay a loan or debt on time.

Deliverables

The tasks you agree to complete as part of an NIL deal.

Depreciation

The loss of value over time of an asset.

Direct Deposit

Electronic transfer of money directly into a bank account.

DM (Direct Message)

Messages sent through social media apps. Often how NIL brands first reach out.

Diversification

Spreading out investments across different types of assets to reduce risk.

Down Payment

The upfront portion of a purchase, like a car or home.

Earned Income

Money received from working, including NIL activities.

Emergency Fund

Money set aside for unexpected expenses.

Endorsement

When you publicly support a brand or product, often in exchange for compensation.

Engagement Rate

A measure of how actively your audience interacts with your content.

Entrepreneur

Someone who runs their own business. NIL athletes are entrepreneurs.

Equity

Ownership in a business, brand, or property.

Escrow

Money held by a third party during a transaction until terms are met.

Exclusivity Clause

A contract clause that prevents you from working with competing brands.

Expenses

Costs related to your NIL business or personal life.

FICA

Federal Insurance Contributions Act, includes Social Security and Medicare taxes.

Financial Aid

Funding to help cover college costs, including scholarships, grants, and loans.

Financial Literacy

Understanding how to earn, save, spend, invest, and protect your money.

Fraud

Any dishonest activity intended to result in financial gain.

I–M

Identity Theft

When someone uses your personal information without permission for fraud.

Income

The money you earn from NIL, jobs, or investments.

Index Fund

A fund that tracks a specific index like the S&P 500.

Influencer

A person with a social media following who can influence opinions or purchases.

Interest

Money paid regularly at a particular rate for borrowed money.

IRS (Internal Revenue Service)

The U.S. government agency responsible for tax collection.

Investment

Allocating money with the expectation of a positive return in the future.

Invoice

A bill sent to a brand for services provided.

IRA (Individual Retirement Account)

A type of investment account for retirement savings.

Legal Guardian

An adult legally responsible for a minor's financial and legal decisions.

Liability

Legal or financial responsibility for your actions or contracts.

Liquidity

How quickly and easily an asset can be converted into cash.

Loan

Money borrowed that must be paid back with interest.

Market Value

The current price an asset can sell for in the market.

Media Kit

A one-page summary of your brand, including bio, social stats, and photos.

Mentor

An experienced person who offers guidance and support.

Monetization

Turning a brand or audience into income.

Mutual Fund

A type of investment where money is pooled and invested in a diversified portfolio.

N–R

NCAA (National Collegiate Athletic Association)

The main governing body for U.S. college sports.

Net Income

What you keep after expenses and taxes are deducted.

NIL (Name, Image, and Likeness)

Your right to profit from your personal brand as an athlete.

Notary

An authorized official who verifies the signing of legal documents.

Partnership

A formal or informal agreement to collaborate with a brand or organization.

Passive Income

Money earned with minimal effort, such as through investments or royalties.

Payment Method

The way you receive money: direct deposit, PayPal, check, etc.

Portfolio

A collection of financial investments.

Principal

The original sum of money invested or borrowed.

Professionalism

Maintaining reliability, clarity, and respect in business interactions.

Red Flag

A warning sign that something may be a scam or bad opportunity.

Return on Investment (ROI)

The gain or loss from an investment relative to its cost.

Revenue

Total income before expenses.

Reinvestment

Using money earned to grow your business, brand, or financial future.

Roth IRA

A retirement account where contributions are taxed now, but withdrawals are tax-free.

S–Z

Savings Account

A bank account that earns interest on deposited money.

Scholarship

Financial aid given for education, which may be affected by NIL income.

Self-Employment Tax

The tax owed by individuals who work for themselves.

Social Media Strategy

A plan for your posting schedule, audience targeting, and brand voice.

Sole Proprietor

Someone who owns an unincorporated business alone.

Sponsor

A company that pays or supports you to promote their product.

Statement Balance

The amount you owe on a credit card at the end of the billing cycle.

Stock

A share of ownership in a company.

Tax Deduction

A reduction in taxable income due to certain expenses.

Term Sheet

A short version of a contract outlining key deal points.

Transaction

Any action involving the movement of money.

Usage Rights

Permissions granted to a brand for how they can use your content.

Verification

The process of confirming a person or brand's identity.

W-2 Form

A tax form showing wages paid and taxes withheld from an employee.

W-9 Form

A tax form that provides your taxpayer information to those paying you.

Wallet App

A digital tool to store payment cards, IDs, and track transactions.

Wealth

The accumulation of valuable resources and assets over time.

Withholding

The portion of income that is taken out for taxes.

Withdrawal Penalty

Fees for taking money out of certain investment accounts early.

Yield

The income return on an investment.

Zero-Based Budget

A budgeting method where every dollar is assigned a purpose, and income minus expenses equals zero.

Pro Tips for Using the Glossary:

- Bookmark or print this page for quick reference.
- Review it before signing contracts or making deals.
- Use it as a study tool to grow your NIL and financial vocabulary.
- Keep adding new terms as you learn and grow.

Full Disclaimer

The contents of this book are provided for **general informational and educational purposes only** and are not intended to be a substitute for professional financial, tax, legal, or investment advice. While every effort has been made to ensure the accuracy, completeness, and timeliness of the material, the author and publisher make no guarantees and assume no responsibility or liability for any errors, omissions, or interpretations.

Readers are advised to seek the guidance of licensed professionals — including but not limited to Certified Financial Planners (CFPs), Certified Public Accountants (CPAs), attorneys, tax advisors, compliance officers, and registered investment professionals — before making any financial decisions or entering into any legal agreements related to Name, Image, and Likeness (NIL) opportunities, banking, credit, investing, taxes, or scholarships.

This book is intended to introduce basic concepts and practical tools around financial literacy, NIL income, student-athlete decision-making, credit building, and wealth planning. However, each reader's financial circumstances, state laws, institutional rules, and eligibility guidelines may vary. The information shared here may not be applicable to every situation or reflect the most current developments, especially as NIL rules and financial regulations continue to evolve.

Nothing in this book constitutes a client relationship, fiduciary duty, or professional recommendation from the author. All examples and case studies are for illustrative purposes only. Any resemblance to actual persons, organizations, or events is purely coincidental unless otherwise stated.

Furthermore, neither the author nor the publisher shall be held responsible for any loss of income, scholarship eligibility, athletic standing, academic consequences, business loss, or reputational damage arising from the use or misuse of this information. Decisions made by the reader based on the content of this book are done at their own discretion and risk.

This book is written with the intent to **educate and empower**, not to advise or direct. Readers under the age of 18 are especially encouraged to review the content of this book alongside a trusted adult, school representative, or family advisor.

By reading this book, you acknowledge and accept full responsibility for your own financial choices and affirm that any actions you take will be done after conducting your own due diligence and, where necessary, consulting a qualified professional.

Made in the USA
Monee, IL
04 November 2026

67386738R00164